40 MOST STREAMED SONGS
FOR UKULELE

ISBN 978-1-5400-5756-3

Visit Hal Leonard Online at
www.halleonard.com

Contact us:
Hal Leonard
7777 West Bluemound Road
Milwaukee, WI 53213
Email: info@halleonard.com

In Europe, contact:
Hal Leonard Europe Limited
42 Wigmore Street
Marylebone, London, W1U 2RN
Email: info@halleonardeurope.com

In Australia, contact:
Hal Leonard Australia Pty. Ltd.
4 Lentara Court
Cheltenham, Victoria, 3192 Australia
Email: info@halleonard.com.au

Believer

Words and Music by Dan Reynolds, Wayne Sermon, Ben McKee, Daniel Platzman,
Justin Trantor, Mattias Larsson and Robin Fredricksson

sulk - ing ___ to the mass - es, writ - ing my po - ems ___ for the few that looked at me,

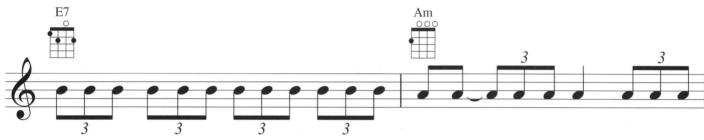

took to me, shook to me, feel-ing me sing-ing from heart - ache, ___ from the pain, tak - ing my

mes - sage ___ from the veins, speak-ing my les - son ___ from the brain, see - ing the

𝄋 Chorus

beau - ty ___ through the... pain! You made me a, you made me a be -

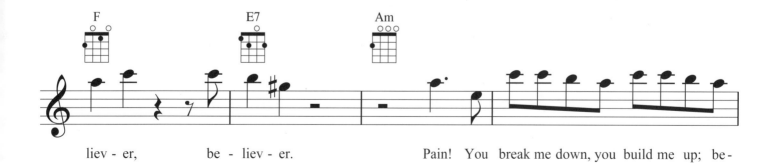

liev - er, be - liev - er. Pain! You break me down, you build me up; be -

liev - er, be - liev - er. Pain! _____ Oh,

let the bul - lets fly, oh, let them rain. _____ My life, my love, my drive, they came from...

To Coda 1

To Coda 2

pain! You made me a, you made me a be - liev - er, be -

Verse

liev - er. 3. Third things third: send a prayer to the ones __ up a -

bove. All the hate that you've heard has turned your spir - it to a dove, oh, ooh, __

your spir - it up a - bove, oh, ooh. _____ I was

Pre-Chorus

chok - ing ___ in the crowd, liv - ing my brain up ___ in the cloud, fall - ing like

ash - es ___ to the ground, hop - ing my feel - ings, ___ they would drown. But they

nev - er did, ev - er lived, ebb - ing and flow - ing, in - hib - it - ed, lim - it - ed, till it broke up and it

D.S. al Coda 1

Coda 1

rained down, it rained ___ down ___ like...

liev - er.

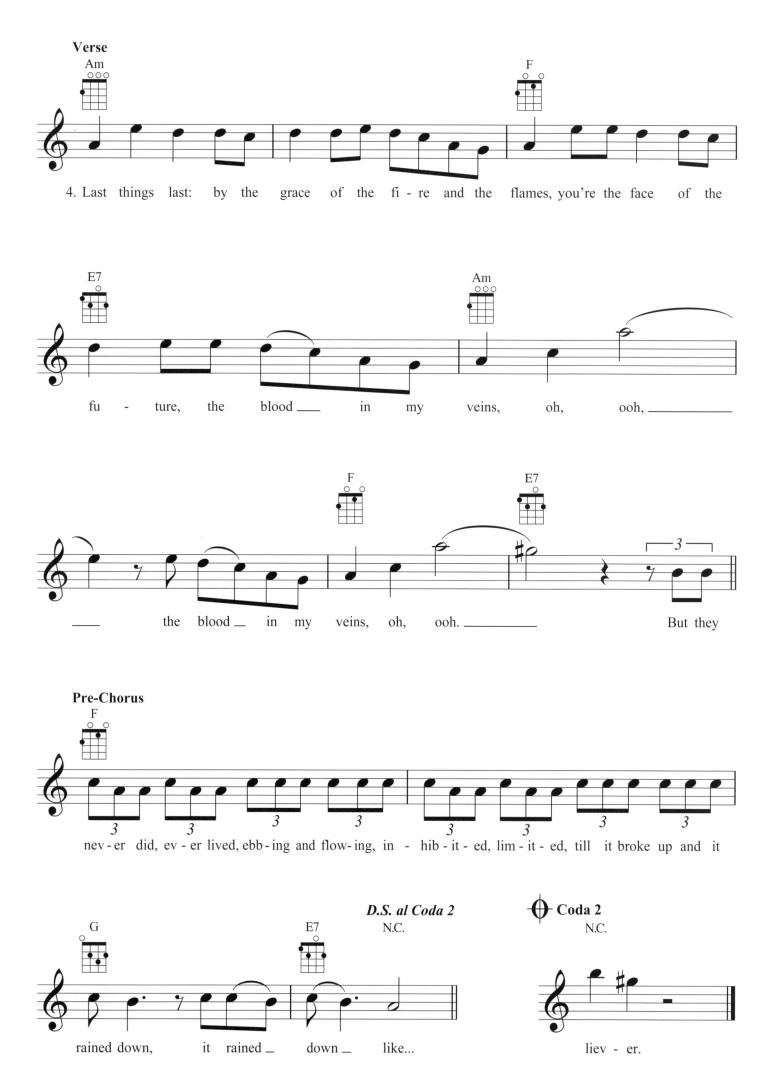

Verse

4. Last things last: by the grace of the fi - re and the flames, you're the face of the

fu - ture, the blood ___ in my veins, oh, ooh, _____

___ the blood __ in my veins, oh, ooh. _____ But they

Pre-Chorus

nev - er did, ev - er lived, ebb - ing and flow - ing, in - hib - it - ed, lim - it - ed, till it broke up and it

D.S. al Coda 2

Coda 2

rained down, it rained __ down __ like...

liev - er.

Eastside

Words and Music by Benjamin Levin, Nathan Perez, Ashley Frangipane, Ed Sheeran and Khalid Robinson

if we put our minds to it. Take your old life, then you put a line through it.

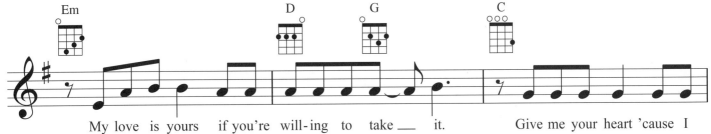

My love is yours if you're will-ing to take ___ it. Give me your heart 'cause I

ain't gon-na break ___ it. So, come a - way, start-ing to - day. ___ Start a

new life to-geth-er in a dif-fer-ent place. ___ We know that love is how all these i - deas

To Coda ⊕

came to be. ___ So, ba - by, run a - way with me.

Verse

Female: 2. Sev - en - teen, and we got a dream ___ to have a fam - i - ly, a house and ev - 'ry-

thing in be - tween. __ And then, oh, sud-den - ly we turned twen-ty-three, and now we got

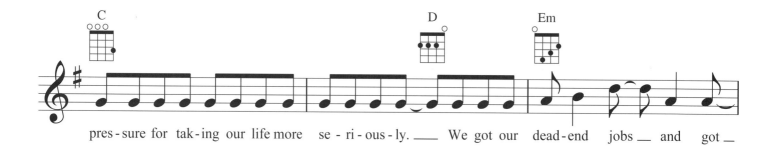

pres - sure for tak - ing our life more se - ri - ous - ly. ___ We got our dead-end jobs __ and got __

__ bills to pay. __ Our old friends __ are now our en - e - mies. And now I,

I'm think - ing back to when I was young, __ back to the day when I was fall - ing in love. __

N.C.

D.S. al Coda

Bridge
Coda

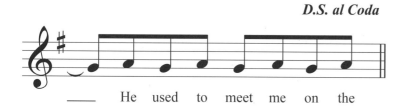

__ He used to meet me on the

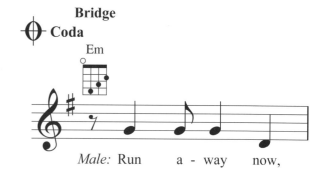

Male: Run a - way now,

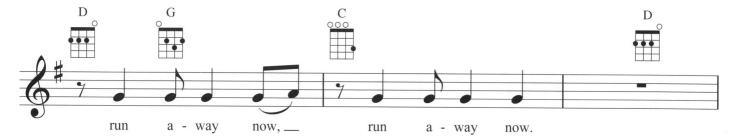

run a - way now, ___ run a - way now.

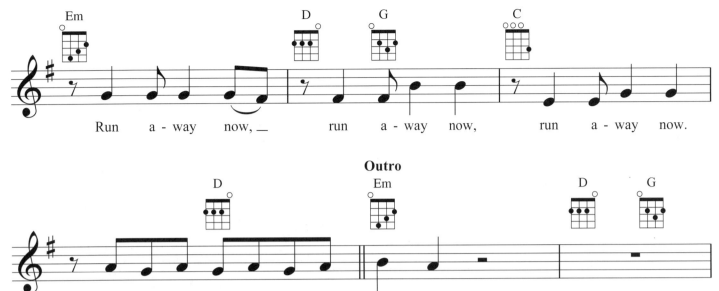

Run a - way now, — run a - way now, run a - way now.

Outro

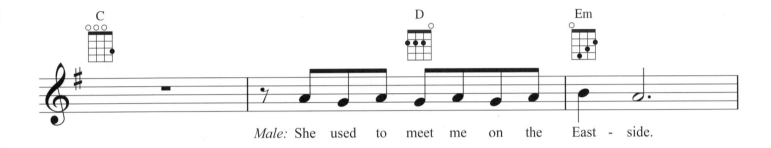

Female: He used to meet me on the East - side.

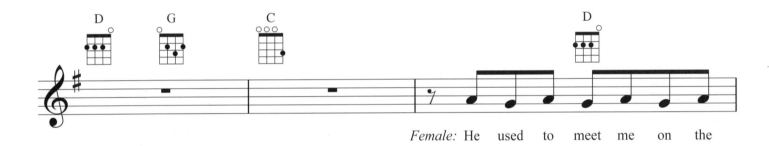

Male: She used to meet me on the East - side.

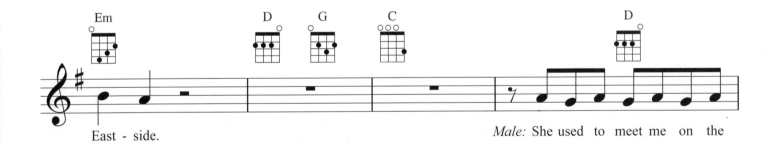

Female: He used to meet me on the

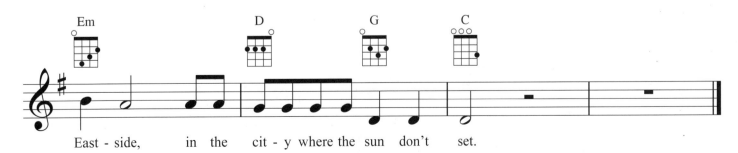

East - side. *Male:* She used to meet me on the

Em D G C

East - side, in the cit - y where the sun don't set.

Despacito

**Words and Music by Luis Fonsi, Erika Ender, Justin Bieber,
Jason Boyd, Marty James Garton and Ramón Ayala**

feel - in' some kind of way. _____ Make me wan - na sa - vor ev - 'ry mo - ment slow -

- ly, slow - ly. _____ You fit me, tail - or -

made love, how you put it on. __ Got the on - ly key, know how to turn it on. __

The way you nib - ble on my ear, the on - ly words I wan - na hear: Ba - by, take it

Pre-Chorus

slow so we can last long. __ Tú, tú e - res el i - mán y yo soy el me -

tal. Me voy a - cer - can - do y voy ar - man - do el plan. Só - lo con pen -

Des - pa - ci - to. Quie - ro des - nu - dar - te_a be - sos des - pa - ci -

- to, fir - mo_en las pa - re - des de tu la - be - rin - to, y_ha - cer de tu

cuer - po to - do_un ma - nu - scri - to. _____

Verse

2., 4. Quie - ro ver bai - lar tu pe - lo, quie - ro ser tu rit - mo,

que le_en - se - ñes a mi bo - ca, tus lu - ga - res ___ fa - vo - ri -

- tos. _____ Dé - ja - me so - bre - pa - sar ___

_____ tus zo - nas de pe - li - gro,   has - ta pro - vo - car tus gri -

_ tos,   y que ol - vi - des tu a - pe - lli - do.

Verse

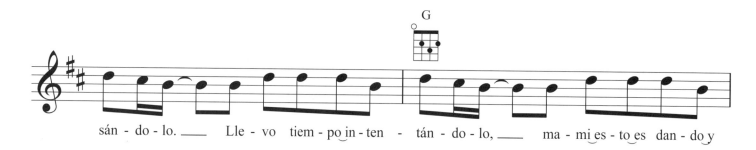

3. Si   te   pi - do un be - so, ven   dá - me - lo. ____   Yo   sé que es - tás pen -

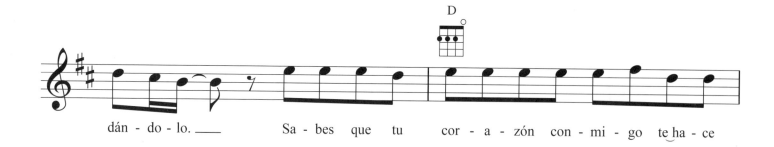

sán - do - lo. ____   Lle - vo tiem - po in - ten - tán - do - lo, ____   ma - mi es - to es dan - do y

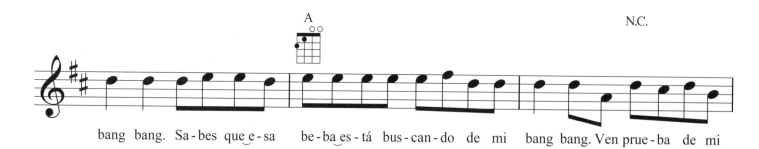

dán - do - lo. ____   Sa - bes   que   tu   cor - a - zón   con - mi - go te ha - ce

bang bang. Sa - bes que e - sa   be - ba es - tá bus - can - do de mi   bang bang. Ven prue - ba de mi

bo - ca pa - ra ver có - mo te   sa - be. Quie - ro, quie - ro, quie - ro ver cuán - to a - mor a ti te

ca - be. Yo no ten - go   pri - sa, yo me quie - ro dar el   via - je. Em - pe - ce - mos

len - to, des - pués sal - va - je.   Pa - si - to a pa - si - to,   sua - ve sua - ve -

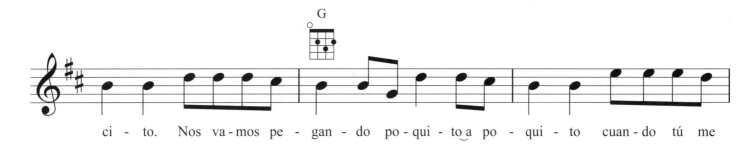

ci - to. Nos va - mos pe - gan - do po - qui - to a po - qui - to cuan - do tú me

be - sas con e - sa de - stre - za. Veo que e - res ma - li - cia con ___ de - li - ca -

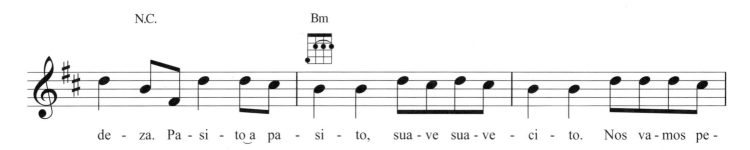

de - za. Pa - si - to a pa - si - to,   sua - ve sua - ve - ci - to.   Nos va - mos pe -

gan - do po - qui - to a po - qui - to. Y es que e - sa be - lle - za en un rom - pe - ca -

be - zas, pe - ro pa' mon - tar - lo a - qui ___ ten - go la pie - za. ¡O - ye!

Coda

D.S. al Coda

Des - pa -

Chorus 2

Des - pa - ci - to. This is how we

do it down in Puer - to Ri - co. I just wan - na

hear you scream - ing, "¡Ay Ben - di - to!" I can move for -

ev - er se que - de con - ti - go. ___ Pa - si - to a pa -

Outro-Bridge

si - to, sua - ve sua - ve - ci - to. Nos va - mos pe - gan - do po - qui - to a po -

qui - to.
Que le en - se - ñes a mi bo - ca, tus lu - ga - res fa - vo - ri -

- tos. _____ Pa - si - to a pa - si - to, sua - ve sua - ve -

ci - to. Nos va - mos pe - gan - do, po - qui - to a po -

qui - to.
Has - ta pro - vo - car tus gri - tos. Y que ol - vi - des ___ tu a - pe -

lli - do. Des - pa - ci - to.

Feel It Still

Words and Music by John Gourley, Zach Carothers, Jason Sechrist, Eric Howk, Kyle O'Quin,
Brian Holland, Freddie Gorman, Georgia Dobbins, Robert Bateman,
William Garrett, John Hill and Asa Taccone

nine-teen six-ty-six, now. Might be o-ver ___ now, but I feel it still.
Might have had your ___ fill, but you feel it still.

Ooh, _____ I'm a

reb-el just for kicks, now. Let me kick it like it's nine-teen eight-y-six, now.

To Coda

Might be o-ver ___ now, but I feel it still.

Verse

Dm

2. Got an-oth-er mouth to feed. _____

F   Gm

Leave it with a ba-by-sit-ter; Ma-ma, call the grave-dig-ger.

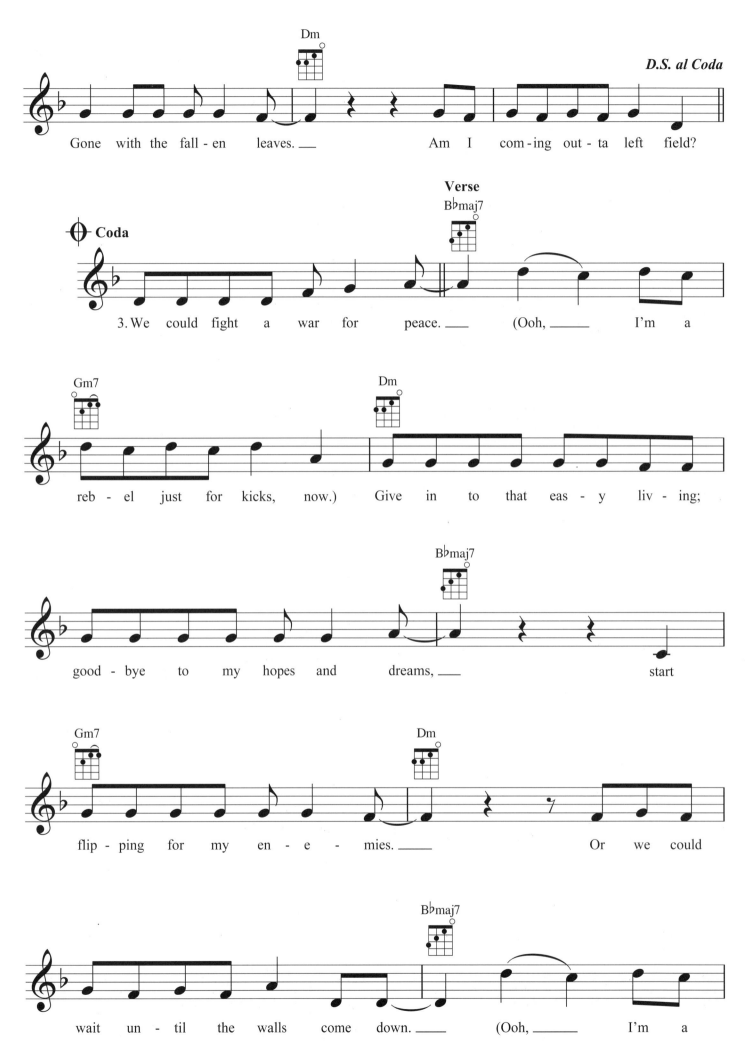

Dm

Gone with the fall-en leaves. ___ Am I com-ing out-ta left field?

Verse
B♭maj7

Coda

3. We could fight a war for peace. ___ (Ooh, ___ I'm a

Gm7   Dm

reb - el just for kicks, now.) Give in to that eas - y liv - ing;

B♭maj7

good - bye to my hopes and dreams, ___ start

Gm7   Dm

flip - ping for my en - e - mies. ___ Or we could

B♭maj7

wait un - til the walls come down. ___ (Ooh, ___ I'm a

reb - el just for kicks, now.) It's time to give a lit - tle to the

kids in the mid - dle, but, oh, _____ un - til _____ it falls, _

_ won't both - er me. (Is it com - ing?

Is it com - ing? Is it com - ing? Is it com - ing?

Is it com - ing? Is it com - ing back?) _

Pre-Chorus

Ooh, _ I'm a reb - el just for kicks. Yeah, your

love is an a-byss for my heart to e-clipse, now. Might be o-ver __ now,

but I feel it still.

Chorus

Ooh, _____ I'm a reb-el just for kicks, now.

{ I've been feel-ing it since nine-teen six-ty-six, now. }
{ Let me kick it like it's nine-teen eight-y-six, now. }

1.

Might be o-ver __ now, but I feel it still.

2.

Might have had your fill, but you feel it still. __

24

Finesse

Words and Music by Bruno Mars, Philip Lawrence, James Fauntleroy, Ray Charles McCullough II,
Christopher Brody Brown, Jeremy Reeves, Jonathan Yip and Ray Romulus

it, you know it. Fel - las, grab your la - dies if your

la - dy fine; tell her she the one, she the one for life.

La - dies, grab your fel - las and let's do this right if you're

on one like me and mine. Yeah, we

got it go - in' on, got it go - in' on. Don't it feel so good to be us to - day? Yeah, we

got it go - in' on, got it go - in' on. Girl, we got it go - in' on. Yeah, we

Girls Like You

Words and Music by Adam Levine, Brittany Hazzard, Jason Evigan, Henry Walter and Gian Stone

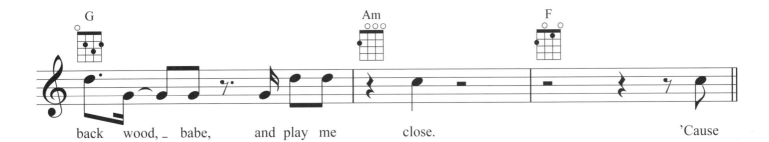

back wood, _ babe, and play me close. 'Cause

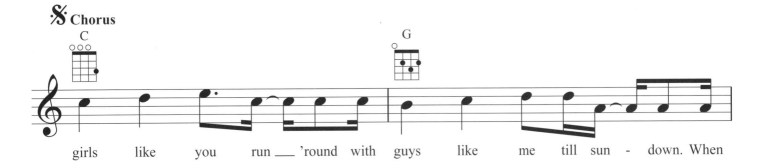

girls like you run __ 'round with guys like me till sun - down. When

I come through, I _____ need a girl like you, yeah __ yeah.

Girls like you love __ fun, and yeah, me too, what I _____ want. When

I come through, I _____ need a girl like you, yeah __ yeah.

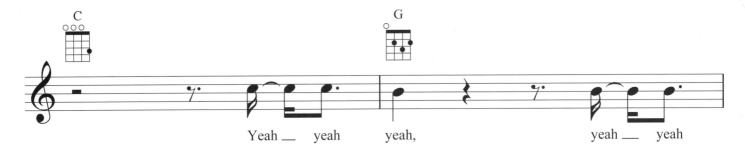

Yeah __ yeah yeah, yeah __ yeah

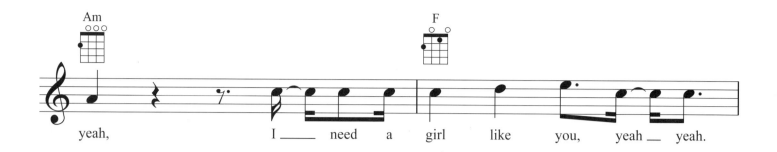

yeah,   I ___ need a girl like you, yeah ___ yeah.

To Coda ⊕

Yeah ___ yeah yeah,   yeah ___ yeah yeah,   I ___ need a

Verse

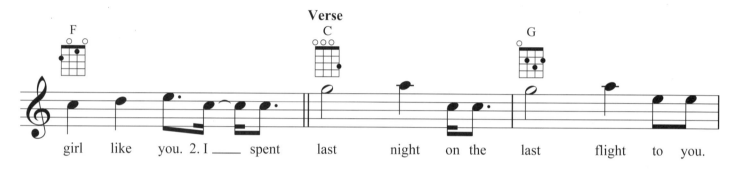

girl like you. 2. I ___ spent last night on the last flight to you.

We took a whole day _____ up tryin' to get

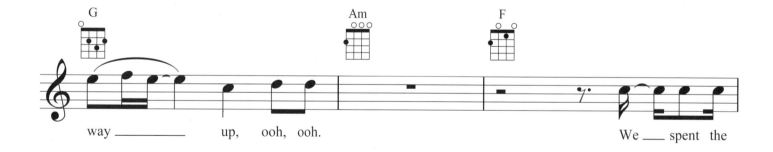

way _____ up, ooh, ooh.   We ___ spent the

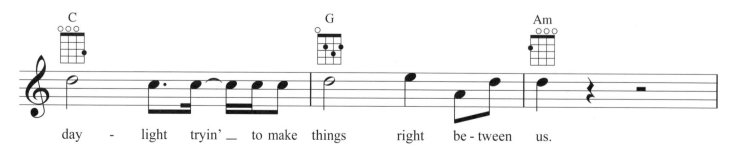

day - light tryin' ___ to make things right be - tween us.

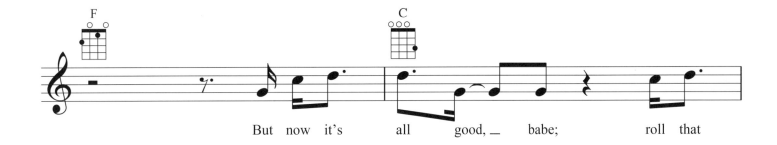

But now it's all good, _ babe; roll that

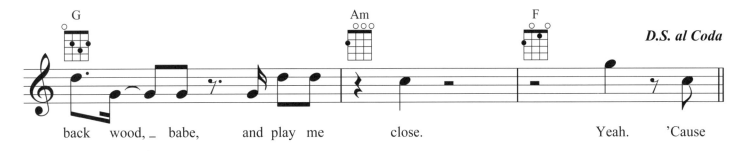

D.S. al Coda

back wood, _ babe, and play me close. Yeah. 'Cause

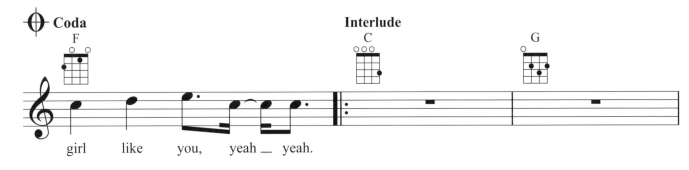

Coda

Interlude

girl like you, yeah _ yeah.

1.

2.

I _ need a girl like you, yeah _ yeah. girl like you.

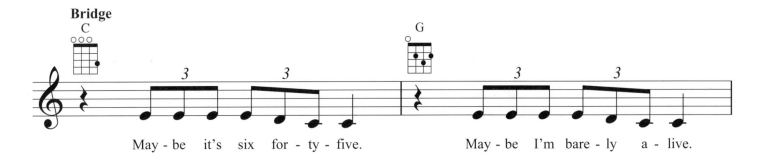

Bridge

3   3   3   3

May - be it's six for - ty - five. May - be I'm bare - ly a - live.

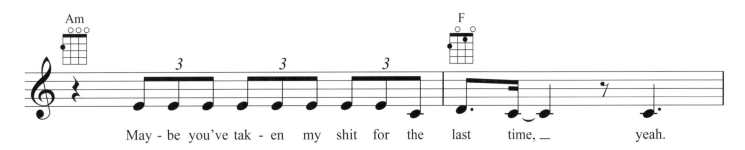

3   3   3

May - be you've tak - en my shit for the last time, _ yeah.

May - be I know that I'm drunk. May - be I know you're the one.

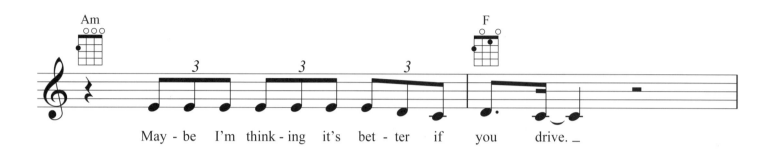

May - be I'm think - ing it's bet - ter if you drive.

Chorus

Oh, 'cause girls like you run ___ 'round with guys like me till sun - down. When

I come through, I ___ need a girl like you, yeah. ___ 'Cause

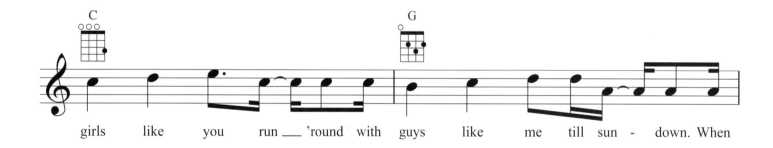

girls like you run ___ 'round with guys like me till sun - down. When

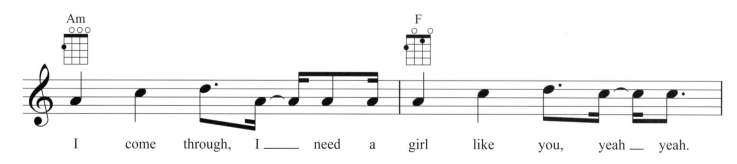

I come through, I ___ need a girl like you, yeah ___ yeah.

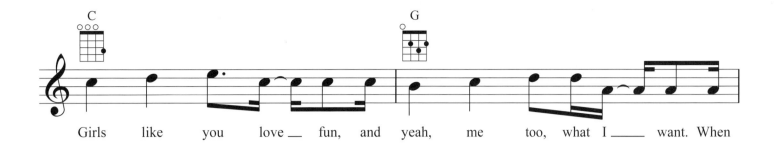

Girls like you love __ fun, and yeah, me too, what I ____ want. When

I come through, I ____ need a girl like you, yeah __ yeah.

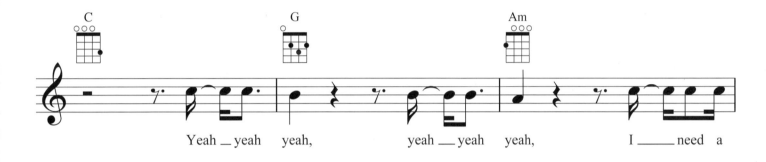

Yeah __ yeah yeah, yeah __ yeah yeah, I ____ need a

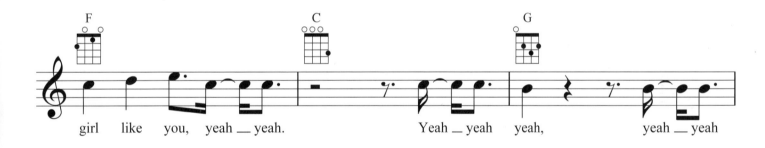

girl like you, yeah __ yeah. Yeah __ yeah yeah, yeah __ yeah

Outro

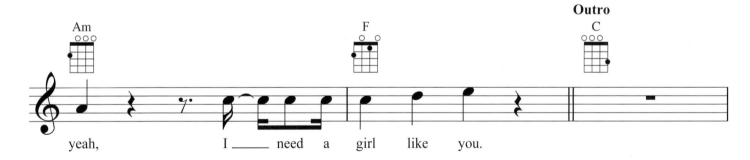

yeah, I ____ need a girl like you.

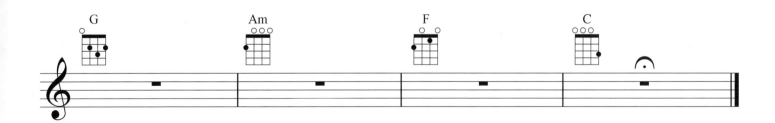

Happier

Words and Music by Marshmello, Steve Mac and Dan Smith

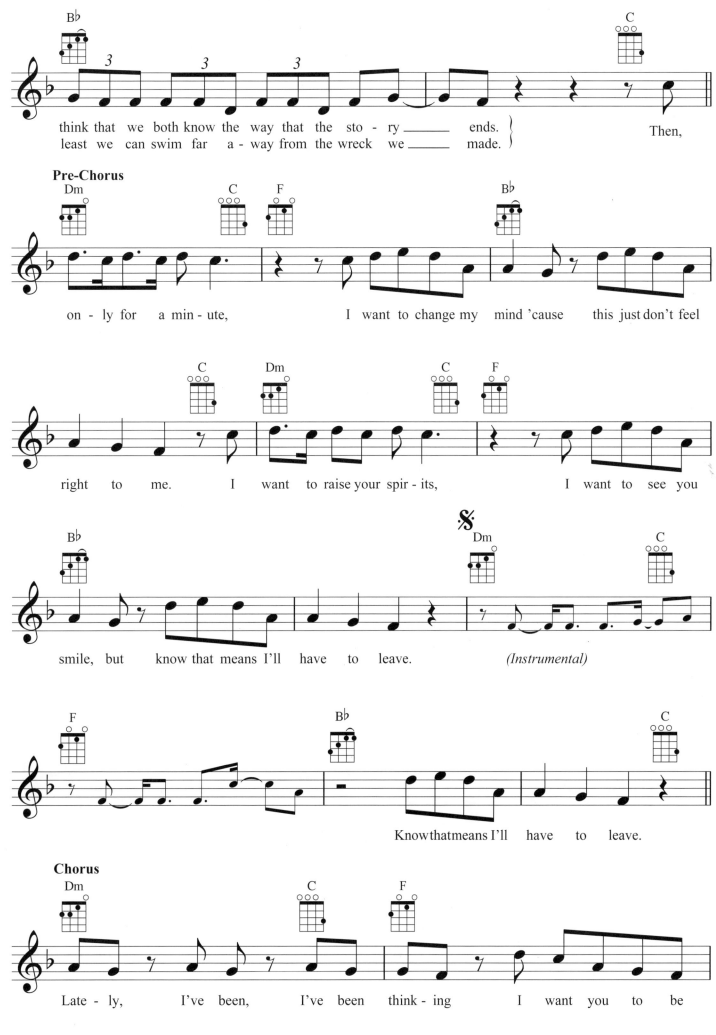

think that we both know the way that the sto — ry _____ ends.
least we can swim far a — way from the wreck we _____ made.

Then,

Pre-Chorus

on — ly for a min — ute, I want to change my mind 'cause this just don't feel

right to me. I want to raise your spir - its, I want to see you

smile, but know that means I'll have to leave. *(Instrumental)*

Know that means I'll have to leave.

Chorus

Late — ly, I've been, I've been think - ing I want you to be

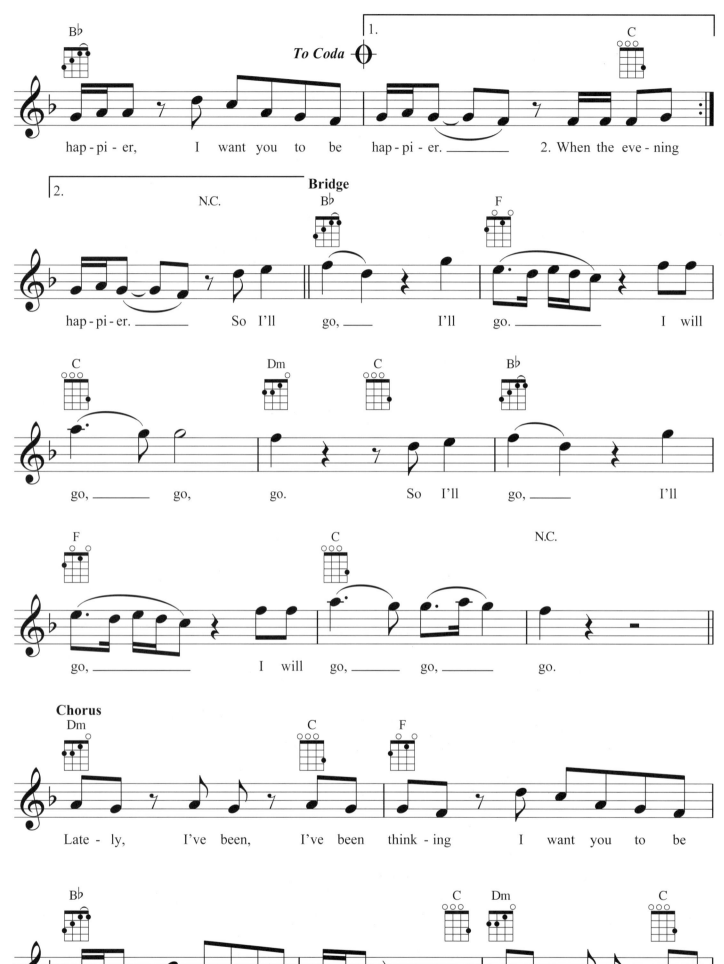

like this,   I   think   that   you'll   be   hap - pi - er,   I   want   you   to   be

Pre-Chorus

hap - pi - er. _____   Then,   on - ly   for   a   min - ute,

I   want   to   change   my   mind 'cause   this   just   don't   feel   right   to   me.   I

want   to   raise   your   spir - its,   I   want   to   see   you   smile,   but   know   that   means   I'll

Outro

D.S. al Coda

have   to   leave.

Coda

hap - pi - er.   So   I'll   go, _____   I'll

go, _____   I   will   go, _____   go,   go.

Havana

Words and Music by Camila Cabello, Louis Bell, Pharrell Williams,
Adam Feeney, Ali Tamposi, Jeffery Lamar Williams, Brian Lee,
Andrew Wotman, Brittany Hazzard and Kaan Gunesberk

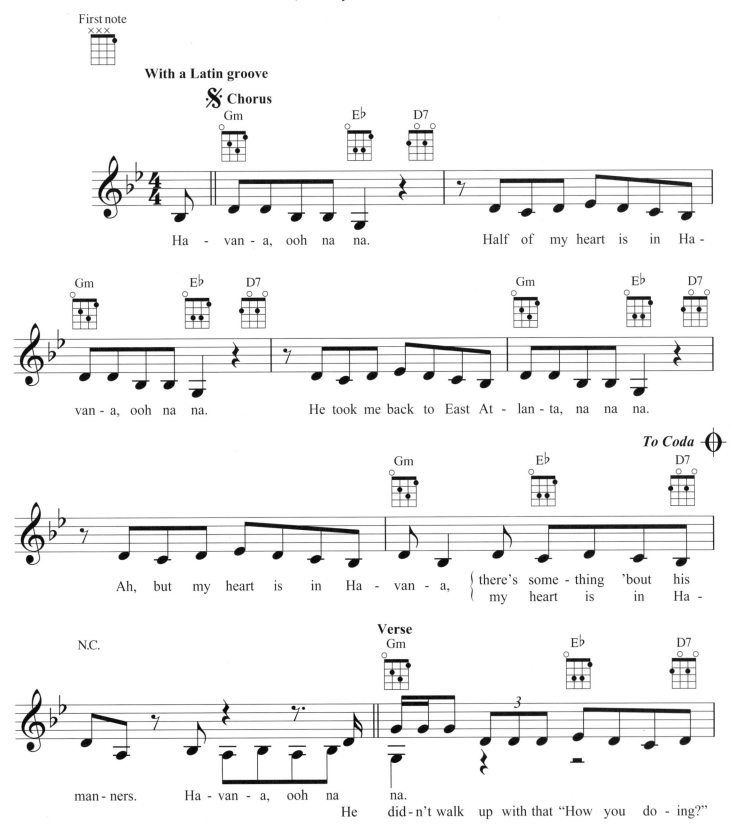

And then I had to tell him I had to go, — oh, na na na na na. Ha-

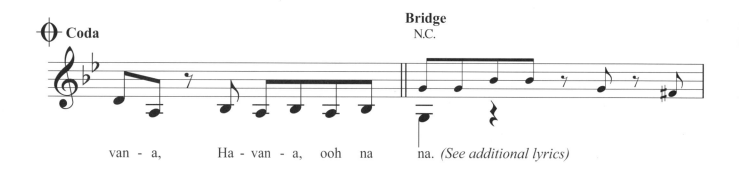

Coda

Bridge

van - a, Ha - van - a, ooh na na. *(See additional lyrics)*

na.   Take me back, back, back.

Ooh. _____   Ooh. _____

_____   Ha - van - a, ooh na na.   Half of my heart is in Ha-

van - a, ooh na na.   He took me back to East At - lan - ta, na na na.

Ah, but my heart is in Ha - van - a,   my heart is in Ha - van - a,   Ha - van - a, ooh na

Outro

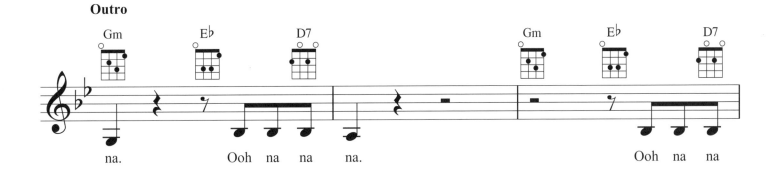

na. Ooh na na na. Ooh na na

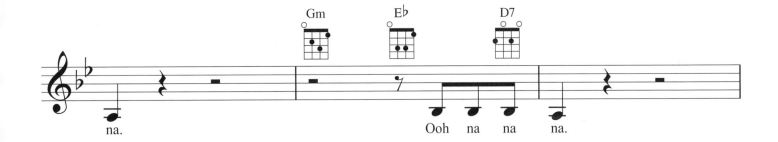

na. Ooh na na na.

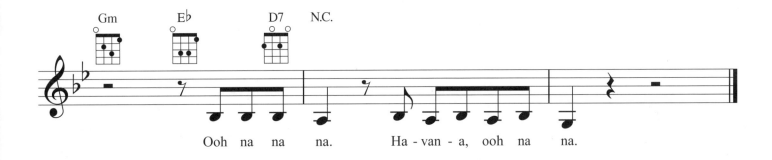

Ooh na na na. Ha - van - a, ooh na na.

Additional Lyrics

Jeffery,
Just graduated, fresh on campus, mmm.
Fresh out East Atlanta with no manners, damn.
Fresh out East Atlanta.
Bump on her bumper like a traffic jam (jam).
Hey, I was quick to pay that girl like Uncle Sam. (Here you go, ay).
Back it on me, shawty cravin' on me.
Get to diggin' on me (on me).
She waited on me. (Then what?)
Shawty cakin' on me, got the bacon on me. (Wait up.)
This is history in the makin' on me (on me).
Point blank, close range, that be.
If it cost a million, that's me (that's me).
I was gettin' moola, man, they feel me.

High Hopes

Words and Music by Brendon Urie, Samuel Hollander, William Lobban Bean,
Jonas Jeberg, Jacob Sinclair, Jenny Owen Youngs,
Ilsey Juber, Lauren Pritchard and Tayla Parx

"Ful-fill the proph-e-cy. Be some-thing great. __ Go make a leg-a-cy."

Man-i-fest des-ti-ny. Back in the days, __ we want-ed ev-'ry-thing, want-ed

ev-'ry-thing. Ma-ma said, "Burn your bi-o-graph-ies.

Re-write your his-to-ry. Light up your wild-est dreams." Mu-se-um vic-to-ries,

ev-er-y day. __ We want-ed ev-'ry-thing, want-ed ev-'ry-thing. Ma-ma said, __

Pre-Chorus

__ "Don't give up. ___ It's a lit-tle com-pli-cat-

- ed.   All   tied   up, _____   no more love, __

__   and   I'd   hate __   to   see __   you   wait - ing."   Had   to   have

Chorus

high,   high   hopes   for   a   liv - ing,   shoot - ing   for   the
high,   high   hopes   for   a   liv - ing.   Did - n't   know __

stars   when   I   could - n't   make   a   kill - ing.   Did - n't   have   a
how,   but   I   al - ways   had   a   feel - ing   I   was   gon - na

To Coda

dime,   but   I   al - ways   had   a   vi - sion.   Al - ways   had
be   that __   one __   in   a   mil - lion.   Al - ways   had

1., 3.

high,   high   hopes. __   Had   to   have

2.

high,   high   hopes. __

Verse

Bb   F   N.C.   Dm

2. Ma - ma said,   "It's up - hill for odd - i - ties.   Stran - ger cru - sad - ers

C   N.C.   Bb   F   N.C.

ain't ev - er wan - na - bes." The weird and the nov - el - ties   don't ev - er change. _ We want - ed

Bridge 1

Dm   Am   Bb

ev - 'ry - thing,   want - ed   ev - 'ry - thing.   Stay up on that

F   Dm   C

rise,   stay up on that rise   and nev - er come down,   oh. _____

Bb   F   Dm

_ Stay up on that rise,   stay up on that rise   and nev - er come

Pre-Chorus

N.C.   F   A+

down.   Ma - ma said, _____   "Don't give up. _____   It's a lit -

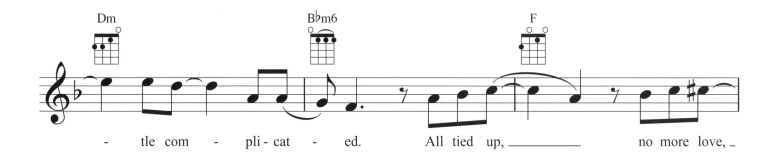

-tle com - pli - cat - ed. All tied up, _____ no more love, _

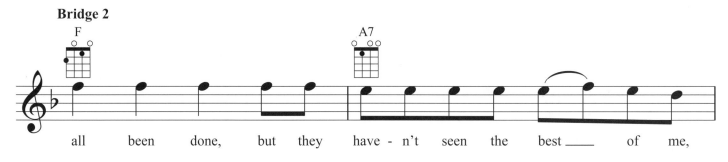

_____ and I'd hate ___ to see ___ you wait - ing." They say it's

Bridge 2

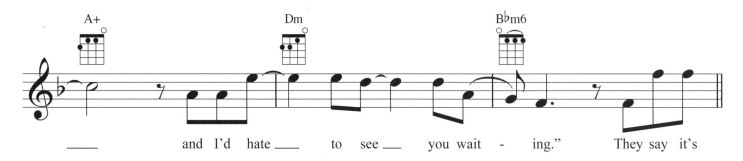

all been done, but they have - n't seen the best ___ of me,

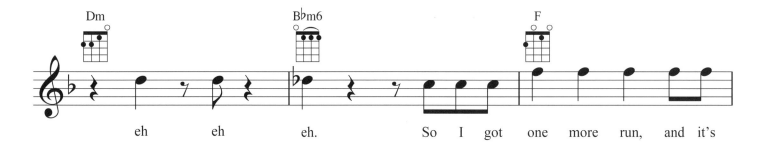

eh eh eh. So I got one more run, and it's

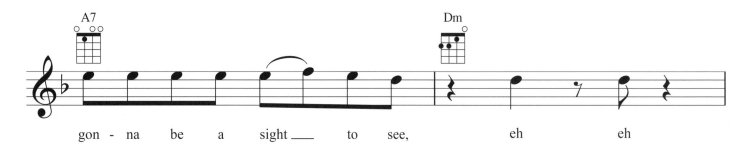

gon - na be a sight ___ to see, eh eh

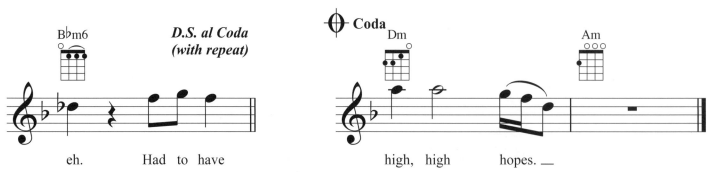

eh. Had to have

high, high hopes. _

Friends

**Words and Music by Anne-Marie Nicholson, Natalie Maree Dunn, Marshmello,
Eden Anderson, Sarah Blanchard, Pablo Bowman, Richard Boardman and Jasmine Thompson**

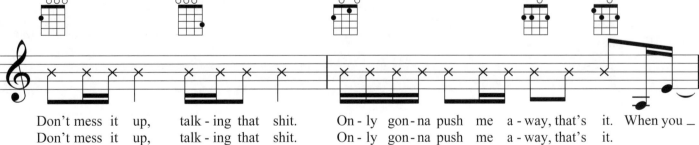

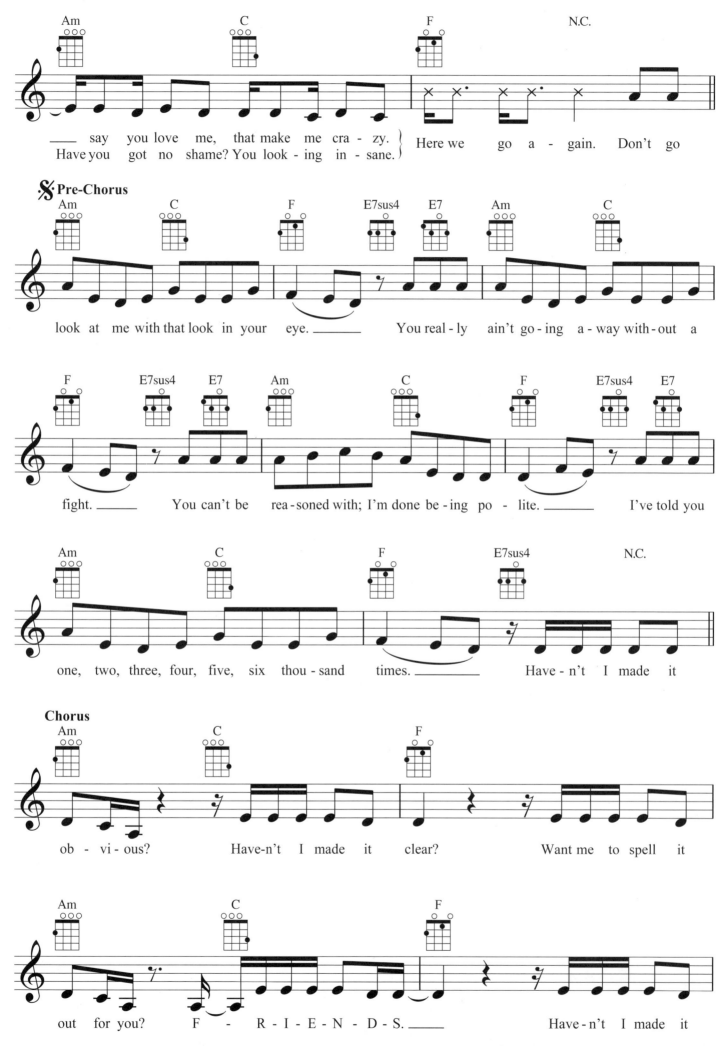

_____ say you love me, that make me cra - zy.
Have you got no shame? You look - ing in - sane. Here we go a - gain. Don't go

𝄋 Pre-Chorus

look at me with that look in your eye. _____ You real - ly ain't go - ing a - way with - out a

fight. _____ You can't be rea - soned with; I'm done be - ing po - lite. _____ I've told you

one, two, three, four, five, six thou - sand times. _____ Have - n't I made it

Chorus

ob - vi - ous? Have - n't I made it clear? Want me to spell it

out for you? F - R - I - E - N - D - S. _____ Have - n't I made it

I Don't Wanna Live Forever

(Fifty Shades Darker)

from FIFTY SHADES DARKER

Words and Music by Taylor Swift, Jack Antonoff and Sam Dew

I Feel It Coming

Words and Music by Abel Tesfaye, Eric Chedeville, Martin McKinney, Henry Walter,
Guillaume Emmanuel Homem Christo and Thomas Bangalter

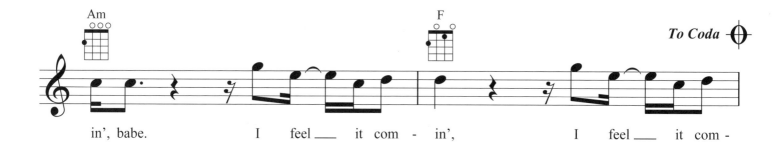

in', babe. I feel ___ it com - in', I feel ___ it com -

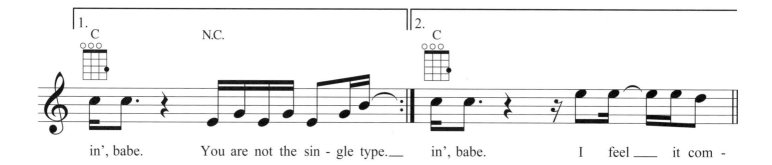

in', babe. You are not the sin - gle type. ___ in', babe. I feel ___ it com -

Chorus

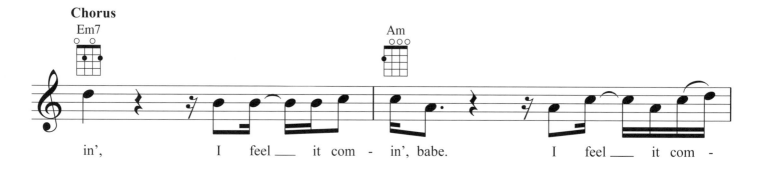

in', I feel ___ it com - in', babe. I feel ___ it com -

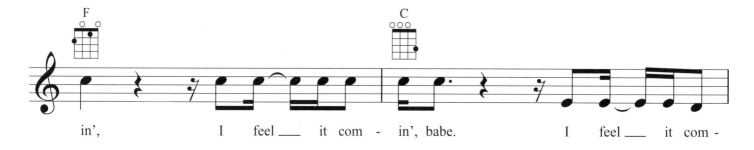

in', I feel ___ it com - in', babe. I feel ___ it com -

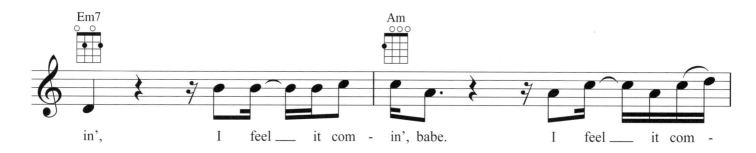

in', I feel ___ it com - in', babe. I feel ___ it com -

D.S. al Coda

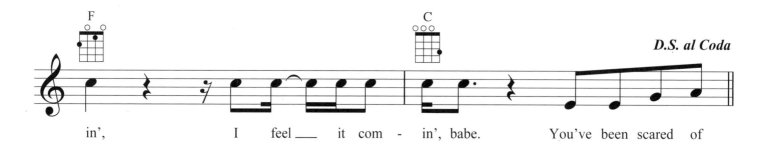

in', I feel ___ it com - in', babe. You've been scared of

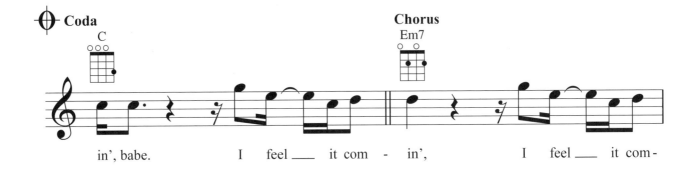

in', babe. I feel ___ it com - in', I feel ___ it com-

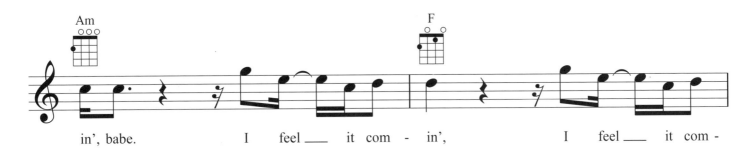

in', babe. I feel ___ it com - in', I feel ___ it com-

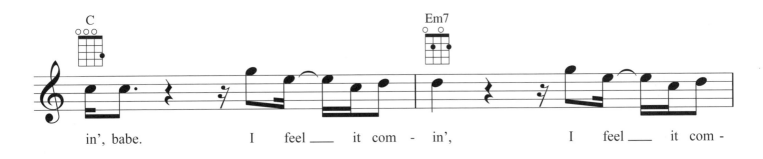

in', babe. I feel ___ it com - in', I feel ___ it com-

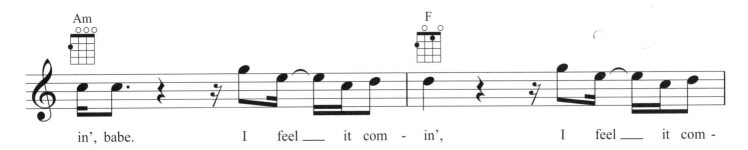

in', babe. I feel ___ it com - in', I feel ___ it com-

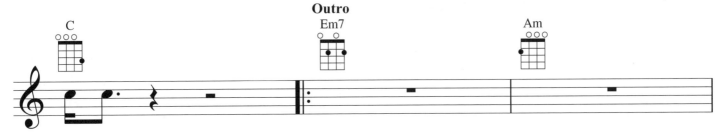

in', babe.

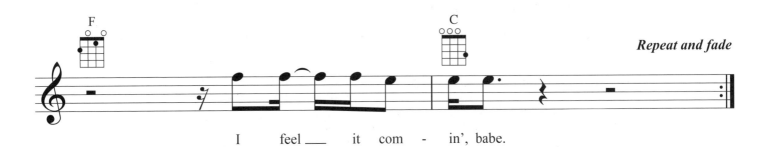

I feel ___ it com - in', babe.

In My Blood

Words and Music by Shawn Mendes, Geoff Warburton, Teddy Geiger and Scott Harris

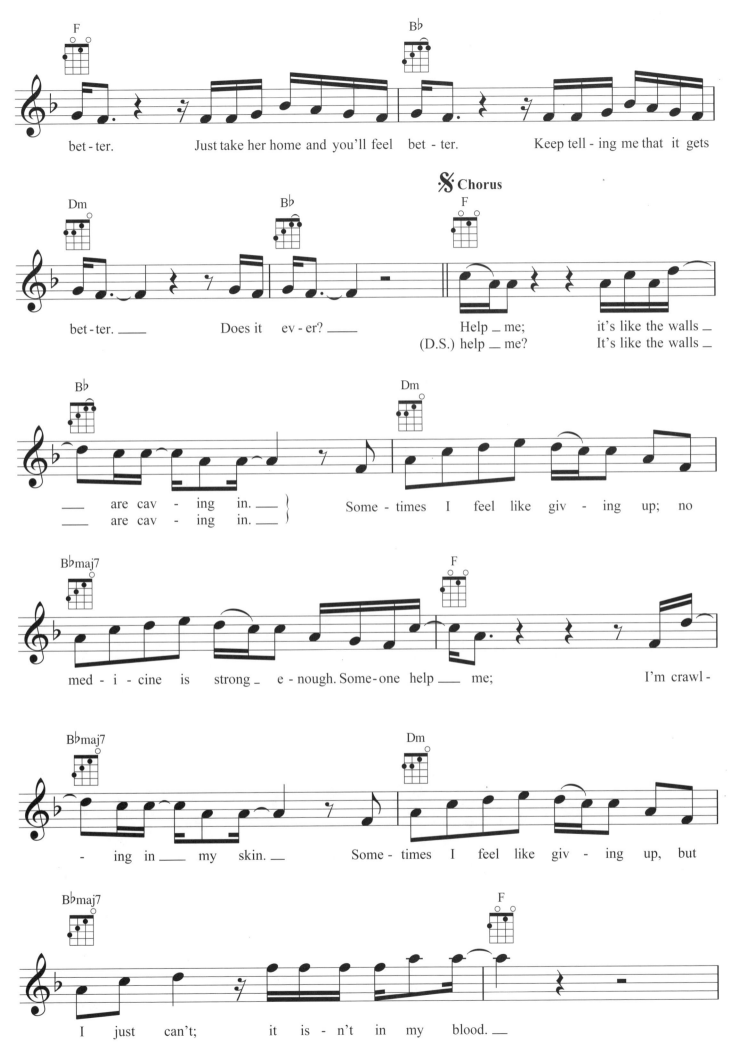

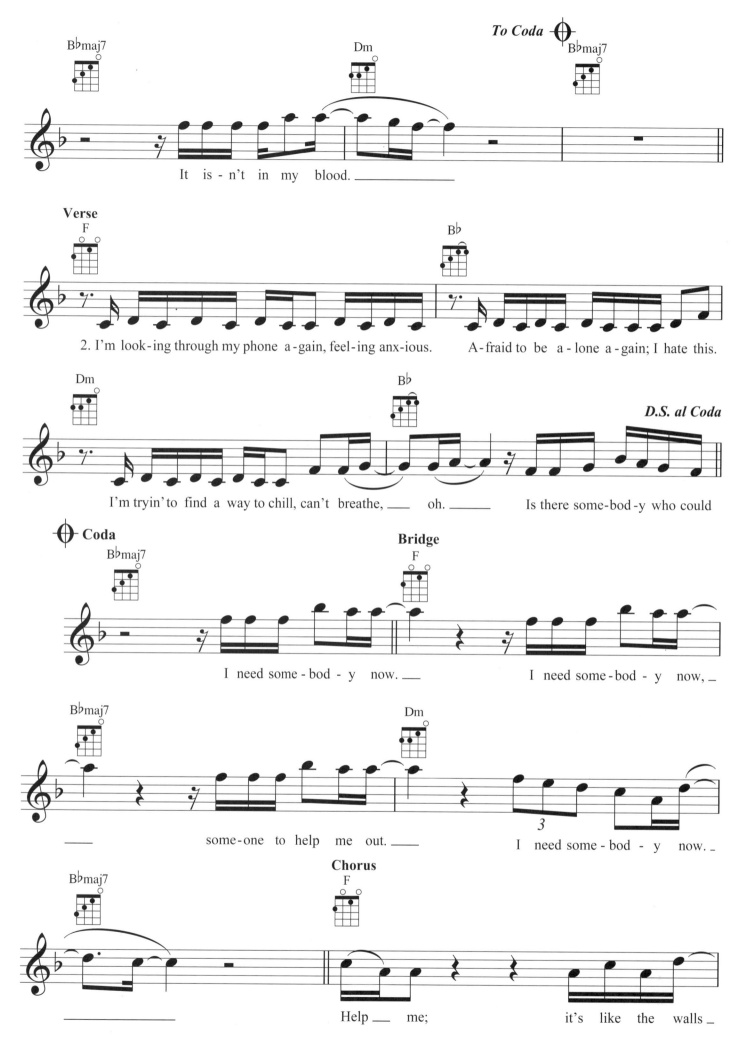

Issues

Words and Music by Benjamin Levin, Mikkel Eriksen,
Tor Hermansen, Julia Michaels and Justin Tranter

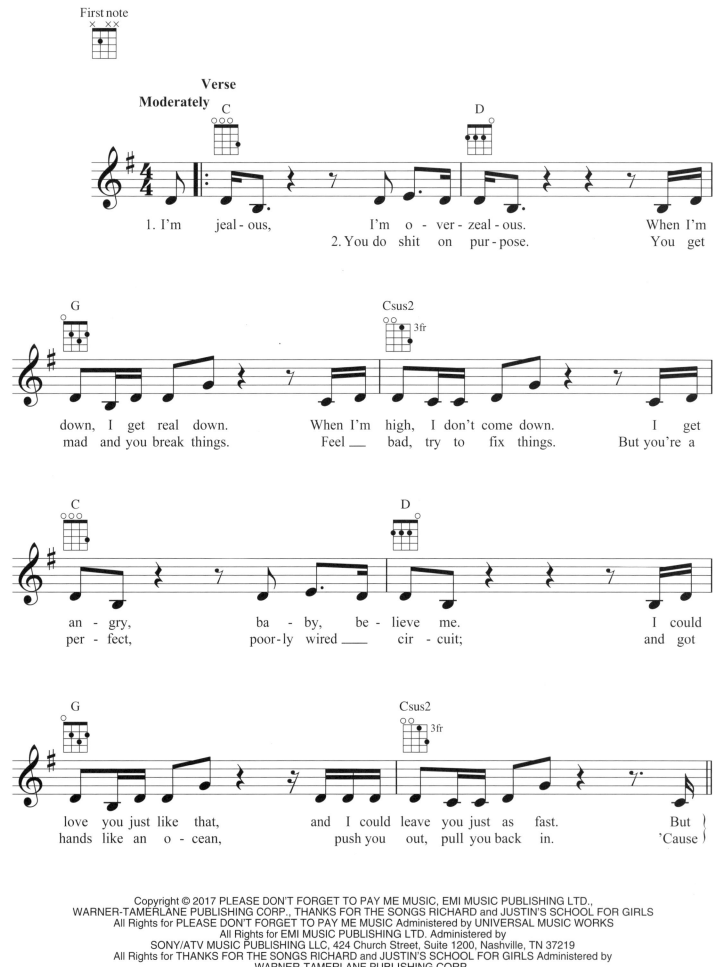

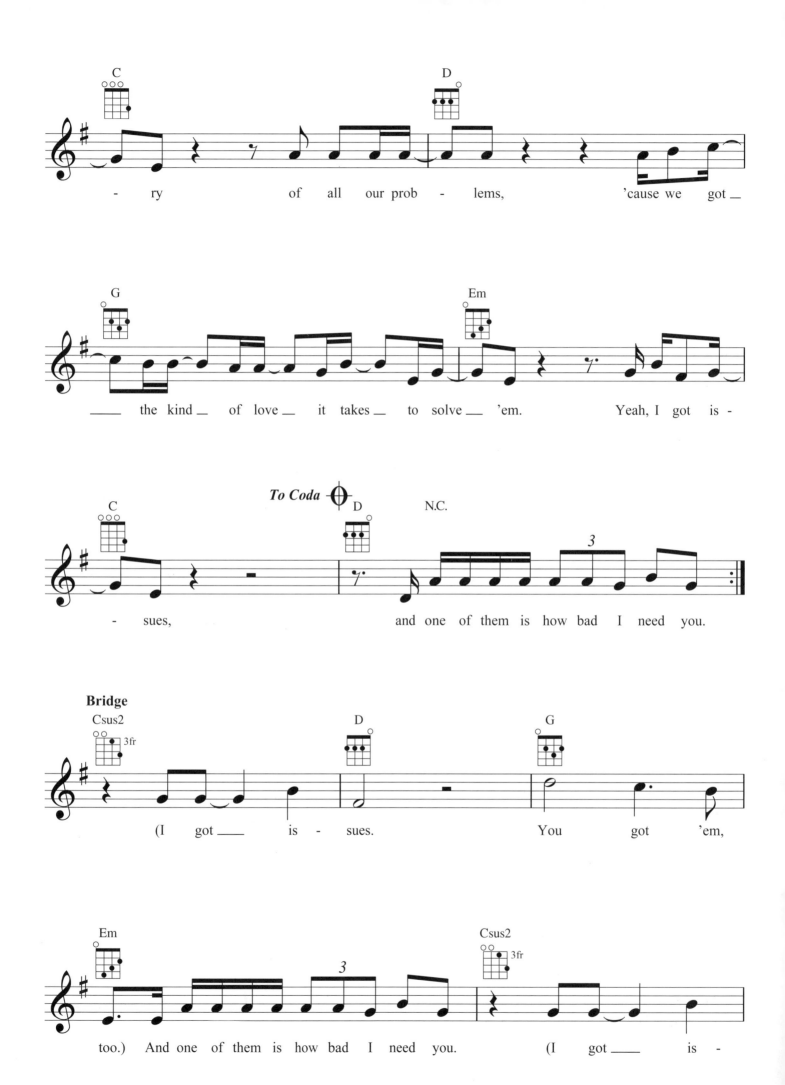

sues.   You   got   'em,   too.   'Cause I   got   is -

Coda

Outro

and one of them is how bad   I need you.   (You   got   'em,

too.)   Yeah, I   got   is -   sues,   (I   got _____   is -

sues.) And one of them is how bad I need you. (You   got   'em too.)   Yeah, I got is -

- sues, (I   got,) _____   and one of them is how bad   I need you.

It Ain't Me

Words and Music by Ali Tamposi, Selena Gomez,
Andrew Wotman, Kyrre Gørvell-Dahll and Brian Lee

Chorus

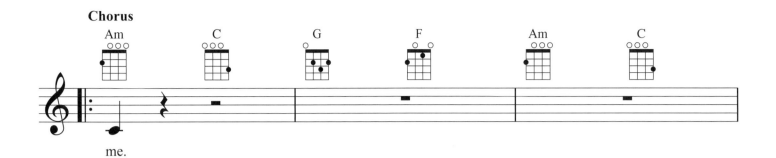

me.

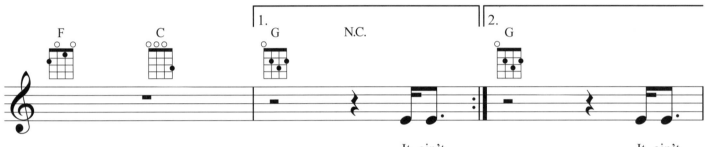

It ain't   me.

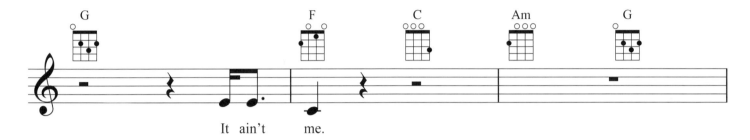

It ain't   It ain't

D.C. al Coda   Coda

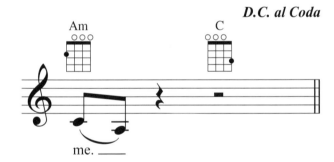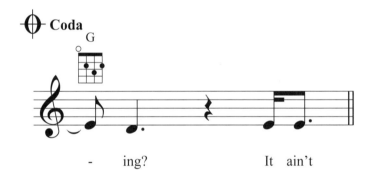

me. _____   - ing?   It ain't

Pre-Chorus

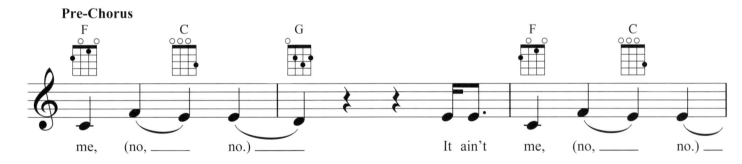

me, (no, _____ no.) _____   It ain't   me, (no, _____ no.) __

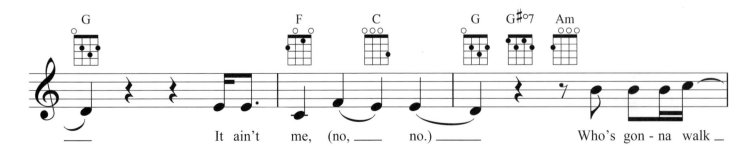

___   It ain't   me, (no, _____ no.) _____   Who's gon - na walk __

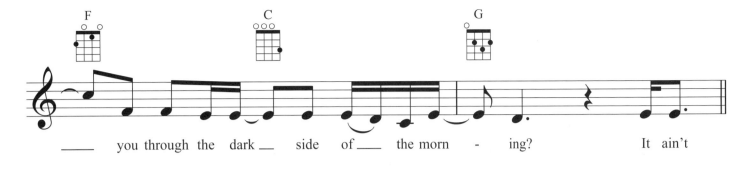

_____ you through the dark ___ side of ___ the morn - ing? It ain't

Chorus

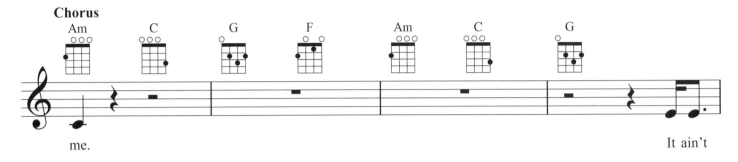

me.   It ain't

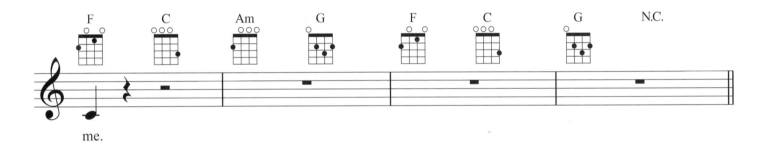

me.

Outro-Chorus

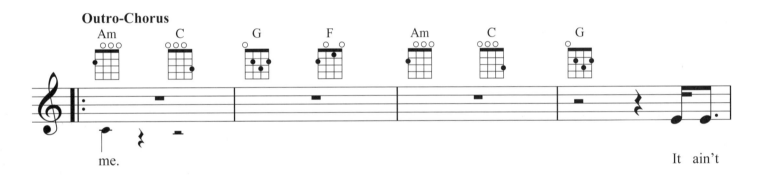

me.   It ain't

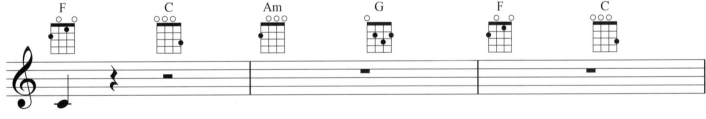

me.

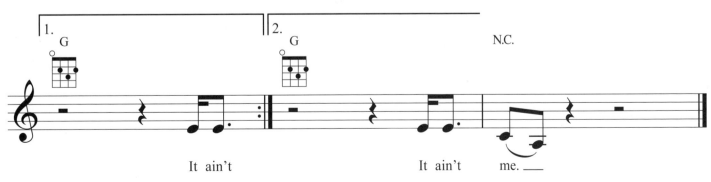

It ain't   It ain't   me. ___

Let You Down

Words and Music by Tommee Profitt and Nate Feuerstein

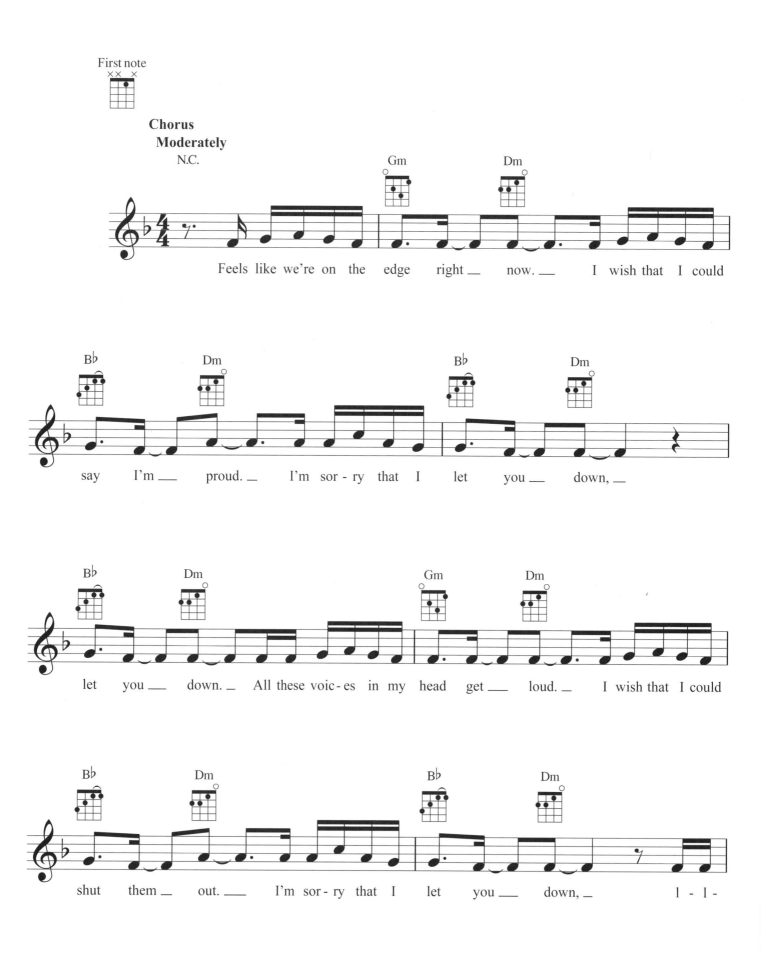

let you _ down. _ Yeah.

Rap 1: *(See additional lyrics)*
Rap 2: *(See additional lyrics)*

Chorus

Feels like we're on the edge right _ now. _ I wish that I could

say I'm _ proud. _ I'm sor-ry that I let you _ down, _ 1 - 1 -

let you _ down. _ All these voic-es in my head get _ loud. _ I wish that I could

shut them _ out. _ I'm sor-ry that I let you _ down, _ 1 - 1 -

Verse

Bb Dm N.C. Gm Dm Bb Dm

let you ___ down. ___ Yeah. **Rap 3:** *(See additional lyrics)*

Bb Dm Bb Dm Gm Dm Bb Dm

Bb Dm Bb Dm N.C.

Feels like we're on the

Chorus

Gm Dm Bb Dm

edge right ___ now. ___ I wish that I could say I'm ___ proud. ___ I'm sor-ry that I

Bb Dm Bb Dm

let you ___ down. ___ Oh, I let you ___ down. ___ All these voic-es in my

Gm Dm Bb Dm

head get ___ loud ___ and I wish that I could shut them ___ out. ___ I'm sor-ry that I

let you __ down. __ Oh, I let you __ down. __ I'm sor - ry.

I'm so sor - ry now. __ I'm sor - ry that I let you __ down. __

Additional Lyrics

Rap 1: I guess I'm a disappointment. Doin' everything I can,
I don't wanna make you disappointed.
It's annoying, I just wanna make you feel like everything
I ever did wasn't ever tryin' to make an issue for you.
But I guess the more you thought about everything,
You were never even wrong in the first place, right?
Yeah, I'm-a just ignore you. Walkin' towards you with my head down,
Lookin' at the ground. I'm embarrassed for you.
Paranoia, what did I do wrong this time? That's parents for you. Very loyal?
Should-a had my back, but you put a knife in it.
My hands are full. What else should I carry for you? I care for you, but...

Rap 2: You don't wanna make this work, you just wanna make this worse.
Want me to listen to you, but you don't ever hear my word.
You don't wanna know my hurt yet. Let me guess; you want an apology probably.
How can we keep goin' at a rate like this?
We can't, so I guess I'm-a have to leave. Please don't come after me.
I just wanna be alone right now.
I don't really wanna think at all. Go ahead, just drink it off.
Both know you're gonna call tomorrow like nothin's wrong.
Ain't that what you always do? I feel like every time I talk to you,
You're in an awful mood. What else can I offer you?
There's nothing left right now. I gave it all to you.

Rap 3: Don't talk down to me. That's not gonna work now.
Packed all my clothes and I moved out.
I don't even wanna go to your house. Every time I sit on that couch,
I feel like you lecture me.
Eventually, I bet that we could-a made this work and probably would-a figured things out.
But I guess I'm a letdown.
But it's cool, I checked out. Oh, you wanna be friends now?
Okay, let's put my fake face on and pretend now.
Sit around and talk about the good times that didn't even happen.
I mean, why you laughin'?
Must have missed that joke. Let me see if I can find a reaction.
No, but at least you're happy.

Look What You Made Me Do

Words and Music by Taylor Swift, Jack Antonoff,
Richard Fairbrass, Fred Fairbrass and Rob Manzoli

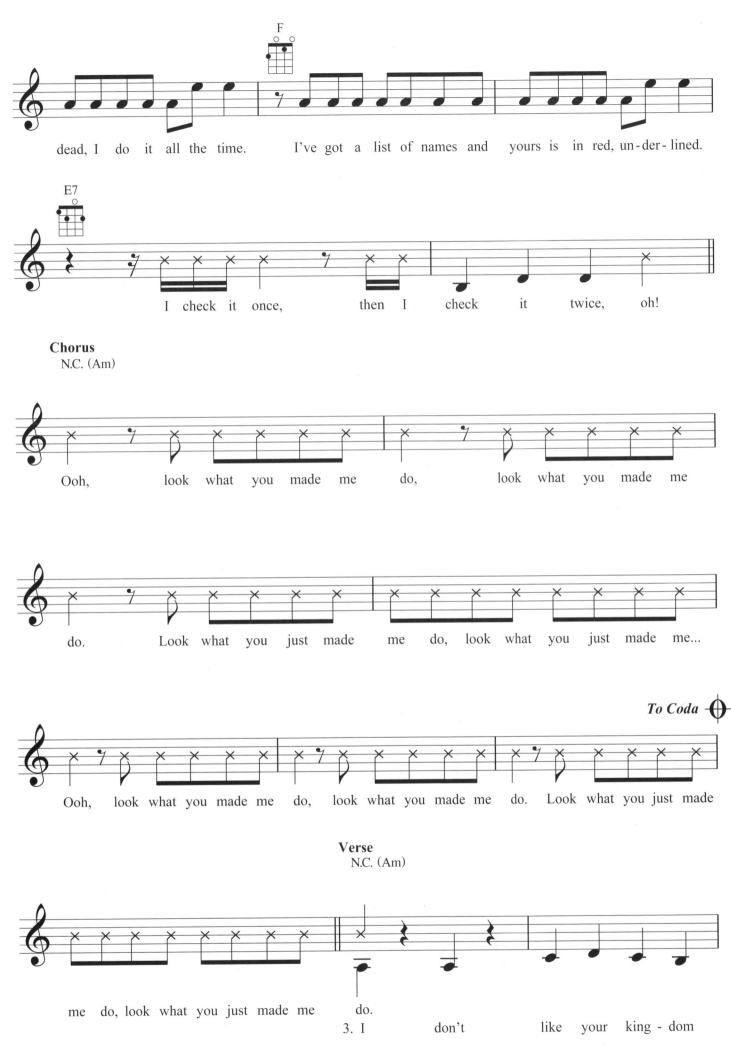

dead, I do it all the time. I've got a list of names and yours is in red, un-der-lined.

I check it once, then I check it twice, oh!

Chorus
N.C. (Am)

Ooh, look what you made me do, look what you made me

do. Look what you just made me do, look what you just made me...

To Coda

Ooh, look what you made me do, look what you made me do. Look what you just made

Verse
N.C. (Am)

me do, look what you just made me do. 3. I don't like your king-dom

keys, they once be - longed to me. You

asked me for a place to sleep, locked me out and threw a feast.

Pre-Chorus

N.C. (Am)

The world moves on, an - oth - er day, an - oth - er dra - ma, dra - ma.
And then the world moves on, but one thing's for sure:

1.

But not for me, not for me, all I think a - bout is kar - ma.
May - be I got mine, but you'll

2.

D.S. al Coda

all get yours.

⊕ Coda

me do, look what you just made me

Bridge

Am

F

do.
I don't trust no - bod - y and no - bod - y trusts me. I'll be the ac - tress

80

1.
E7

star - ring   in   your   bad   dreams.

2.
E7

star - ring   in   your   bad   dreams.

Am

I   don't   trust   no - bod - y   and   no - bod - y   trusts   me.

F

I'll   be   the   ac - tress

1.
E7

star - ring   in   your   bad   dreams.

2.
E7

star - ring   in   your   bad   dreams!

Interlude
Am

Am7   F

(Spoken:) "I'm sorry, the old Taylor can't come to the phone right now.

E7   N.C.

Why?   *Oh,*   *'cause she's dead!"*

Outro-Chorus

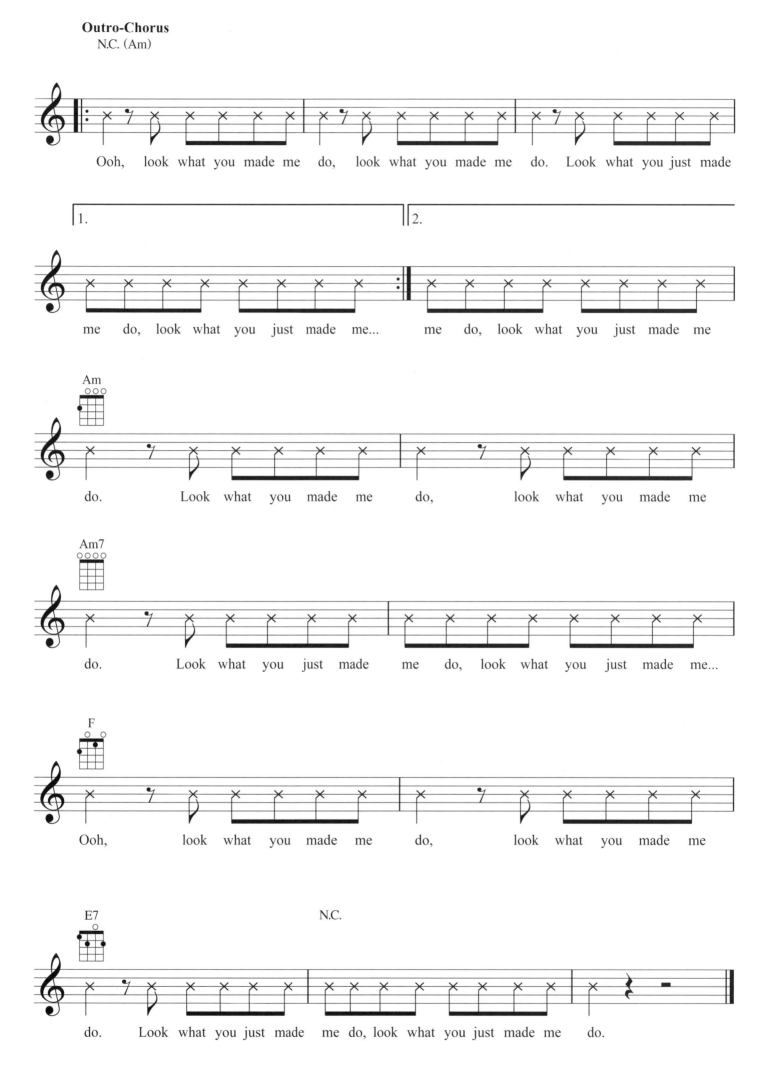

Sorry Not Sorry

Words and Music by Demitria Lovato, Sean Douglas, Warren Felder, William Simmons and Trevor Brown

sor - ry.) Be - ing so bad ____ got me feel - in' so ____ good, _ show - ing you up _

____ like I knew that I would. _ Ba - by, I'm sor - ry. (I'm not

sor - ry.) Ba - by, I'm sor - ry. (I'm not sor - ry.) Feel - ing in - spi -

To Coda 1

To Coda 2

- red 'cause the ta - bles have _ turned. _ Yeah, I'm on fi - re and I know that it ____

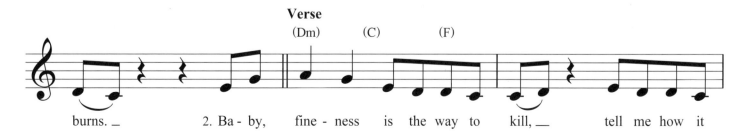

Verse

(Dm) (C) (F)

burns. _ 2. Ba - by, fine - ness is the way to kill, ____ tell me how it

feel, but it's such a bit - ter pill. __ And, yeah, I know you __ thought you had

big - ger, bet - ter things, _ bet right now this stings. (Wait a min - ute.) 'Cause the

grass is green - er un - der me, __ bright as tech - ni - col - or, I can tell that you can

see. _ And, yeah, I know how _ bad it _____ must hurt _ to see ___ me like

D.S. al Coda 1

this, but it gets worse. (Wait a min - ute.) Now,

Coda 1

burns. _

Lucid Dreams

Words and Music by Jarad Higgins, Dominic Miller, Gordon Sumner, Danny Snodgrass Jr. and Nicholas Mira

-ter one. I won't let you for-get me.

2. ____ the one. Lis-ten-ing to my heart in-stead of my head. ____

____ You found an-oth-er one, but I am the bet-

Verse

-ter one. I won't let you for-get me. 1. You left __ me fall-ing __ and

land-ing __ in-side my __ grave. __ I know __ that you want __ me

dead. __ I take __ pre-scrip-tions __ to

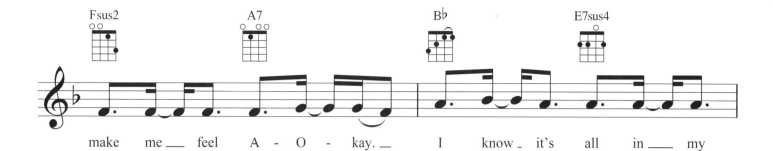

make me __ feel A - O - kay. __ I know __ it's all in __ my

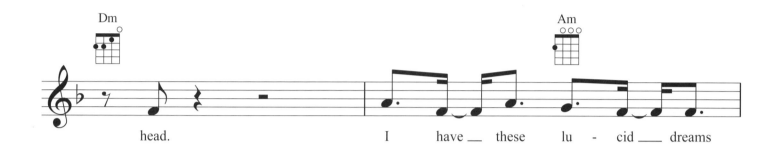

head. I have __ these lu - cid __ dreams

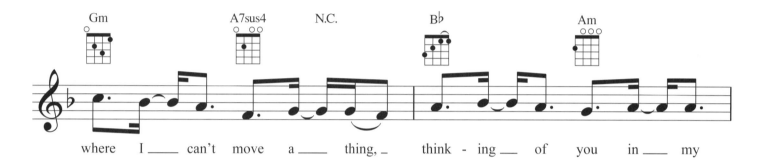

where I __ can't move a __ thing, __ think - ing __ of you in __ my

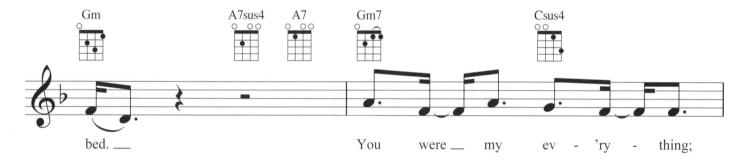

bed. __ You were __ my ev - 'ry - thing;

thoughts of __ a wed - ding __ ring. Now I'm __ just bet - ter __ off __

Bridge

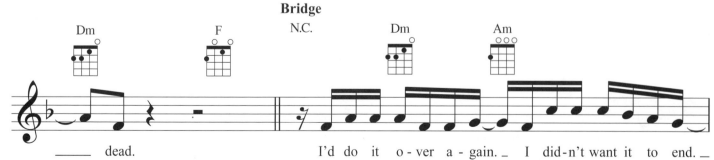

__ dead. I'd do it o - ver a - gain. __ I did-n't want it to end. __

Outro

Did this shit in the past, ___ but I want it to last. ___

___ You were made out of plas - tic, fake. I was tan-gled up in your dras - tic ways. ___

Who knew e - vil girls ___ had the pret - ti - est face?

Eas - i - er said ___ than done. I thought you were ___

___ in-stead of my head. ___ You found an - oth -

- er one. I won't let you for - get me.

93

Meant to Be

Words and Music by Bleta Rexha, Josh Miller, Tyler Hubbard and David Garcia

As long ___ as you're right here ___ next to me, ___ ev-'ry-thing's ___

Chorus

___ gon-na be al-right. ___ If it's meant to be, it-'ll be, ___

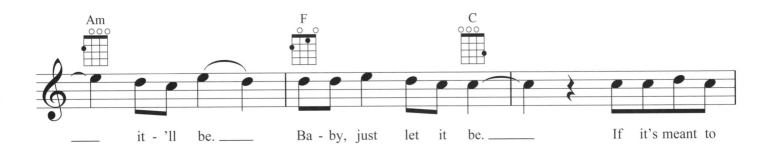

___ it-'ll be. ___ Ba-by, just let it be. _____ If it's meant to

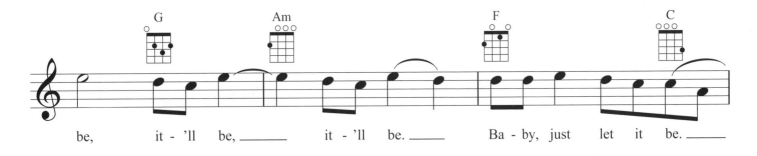

be, it-'ll be, _____ it-'ll be. ___ Ba-by, just let it be. ___

___ So, won't you ride with me, ride with me?

See where this thing goes. If it's meant to be, it-'ll be, ___

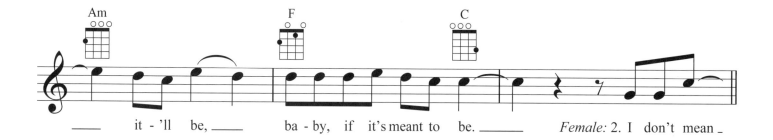

it - 'll be, _____ ba - by, if it's meant to be. _____ *Female:* 2. I don't mean _

Verse

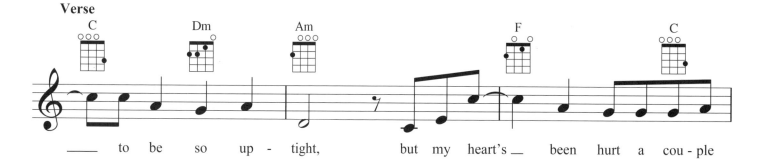

_____ to be so up - tight, but my heart's _____ been hurt a cou - ple

times by a cou - ple guys _____ that did - n't treat me right. I ain't gon - na

lie, ain't gon - na lie. _____ 'Cause I'm tired _____ of the fake love.

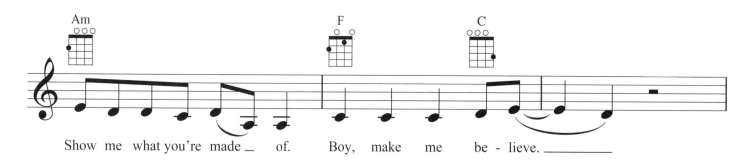

Show me what you're made _ of. Boy, make me be - lieve. _____

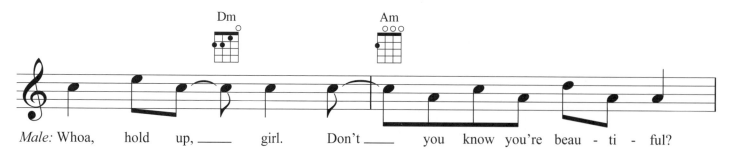

Male: Whoa, hold up, _____ girl. Don't _____ you know you're beau - ti - ful?

Outro-Chorus

The Middle

Words and Music by Sarah Aarons, Marcus Lomax, Jordan Johnson, Anton Zaslavski, Kyle Trewartha, Michael Trewartha and Stefan Johnson

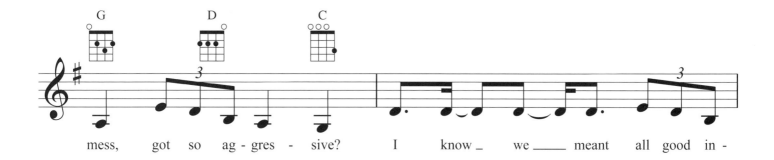

mess, got so ag - gres - sive? I know __ we ___ meant all good in -

Pre-Chorus

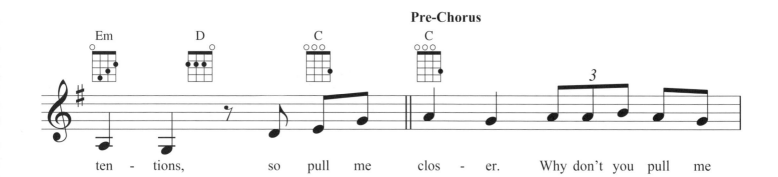

ten - tions, so pull me clos - er. Why don't you pull me

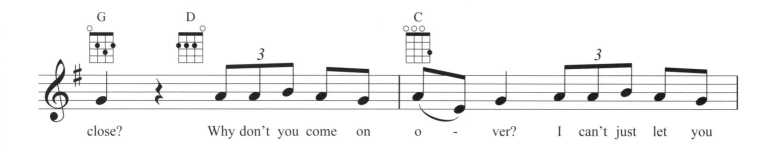

close? Why don't you come on o - ver? I can't just let you

D.S. al Coda

go. __ Oh.

Bridge
Coda

Look-ing at you, I can't lie, just pour-ing out ad-

mis - sion, __ re - gard - less of my ob - jec - tion. __ Oh, oh,

and it's not a - bout my pride. I need you on my

skin, just __ come o - ver, pull me in, just... _____ Oh, __

Chorus

ba - by, why don't you just meet me in the

mid - dle? I'm los - ing my mind just a lit - tle. So,

why don't you just meet me in the mid - dle, in the

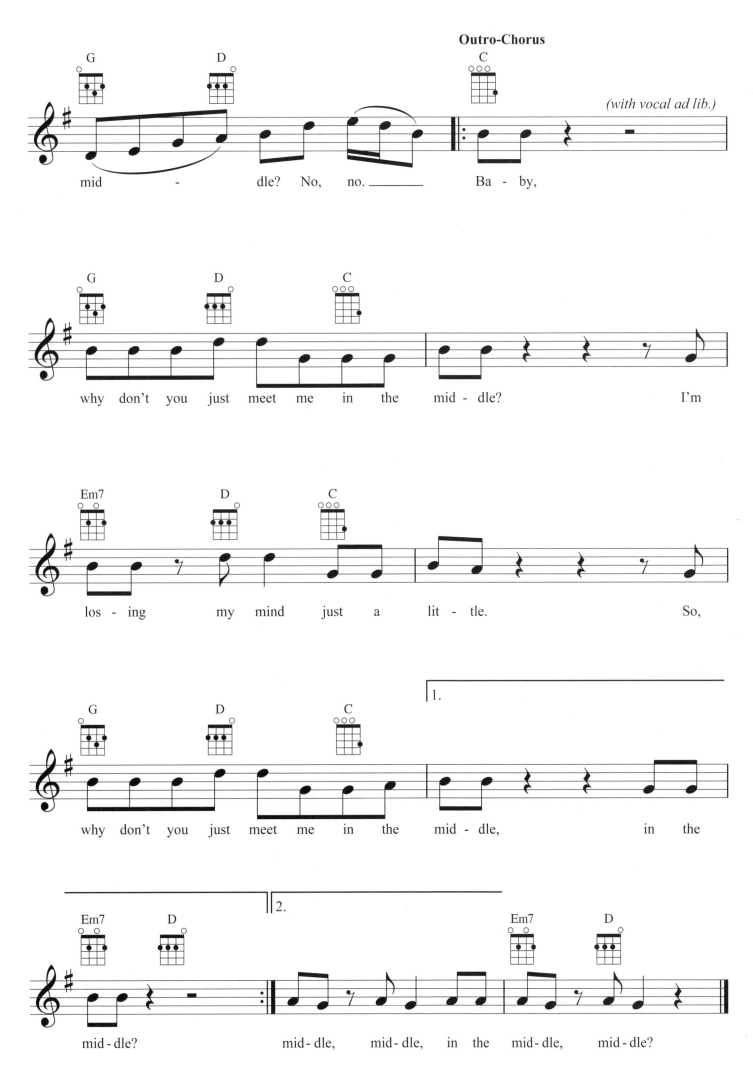

New Rules

Words and Music by Caroline Ailin, Ian Kirkpatrick and Emily Warren Schwartz

no - bod-y else. ___ But my love, _____ he ___

___ does-n't love me, so I tell my-self, ___ I tell my-self: ___

Chorus

One, don't pick up the phone; _ you know he's on - ly call-ing 'cause he's drunk and a-lone.

Two, don't let him in; ___ you'll have to kick him out a - gain. _

Three, don't be his friend; _ you know you're gon-na wake up in his bed in the morn - ing, _

___ and if you're un-der him, ___ you ain't get-tin' o - ver ___ him.

Eat, sleep _ and breathe it, ___ re - hearse and ___ re - peat it, ___ 'cause

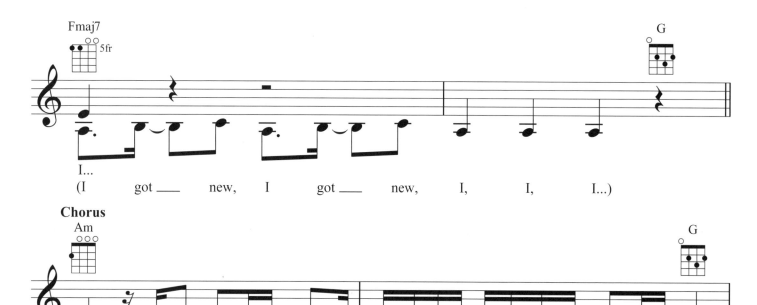

I...
(I got ___ new, I got ___ new, I, I, I...)

Chorus

One, don't pick up the phone; _ you know he's on - ly call - ing 'cause he's drunk and a - lone.

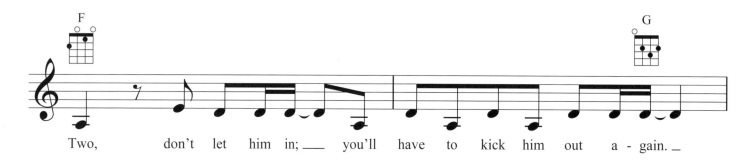

Two, don't let him in; ___ you'll have to kick him out a - gain. _

Three, don't be his friend; _ you know you're gon - na wake up in his bed in the morn - ing, ___

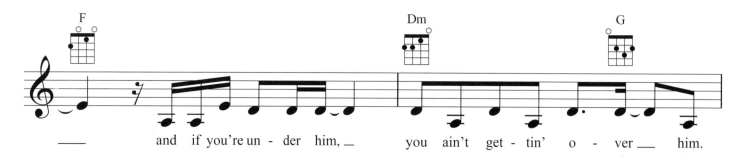

___ and if you're un - der him, _ you ain't get - tin' o - ver ___ him.

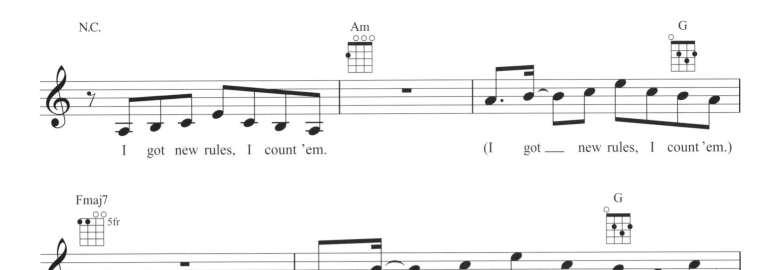

I got new rules, I count 'em.　　　(I　got __ new rules, I count 'em.)

(I　got - ta tell them to my - self.)

(I　got __ new rules, I count 'em.)

Outro

Don't let him in, ___ don't let him in, ___ don't,

(I　got - ta tell them to my - self.)

don't, don't, don't.　Don't be his friend, _ don't be his friend, _ don't,

don't, don't, don't.　Don't

don't, don't. You're get - ting o - ver him.

Perfect

Words and Music by Ed Sheeran

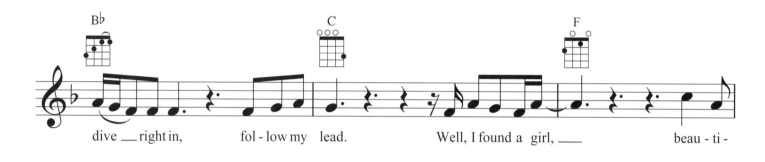

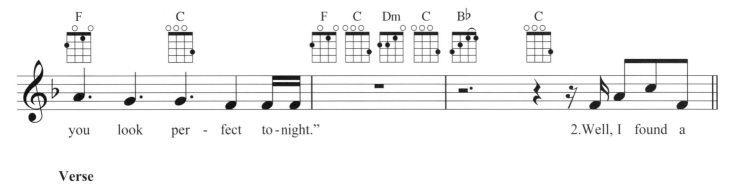

you look per - fect to - night." 2.Well, I found a

Verse

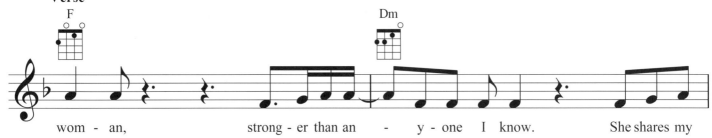

wom - an, strong - er than an - y - one I know. She shares my

dreams; I hope _ that some-day I'll share her home. _____ I found a love _

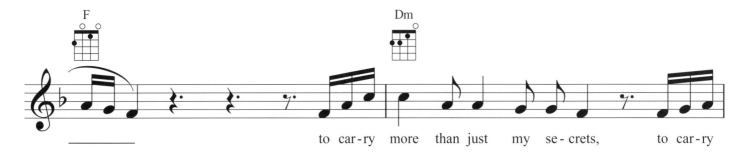

_____ to car - ry more than just my se - crets, to car - ry

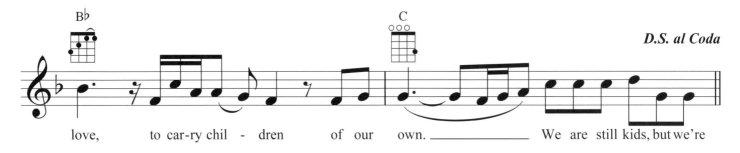

D.S. al Coda

love, to car - ry chil - dren of our own. _____ We are still kids, but we're

Coda   **Interlude**

you look per - fect to - night."

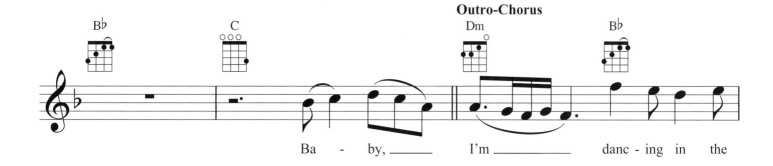

Ba - by, _____ I'm _____ danc - ing in the

dark   with you   be - tween   my   arms.   Bare - foot on the

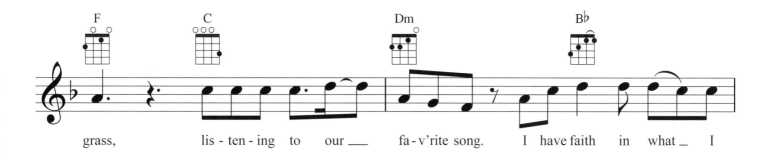

grass,   lis - ten - ing to our ___ fa - v'rite song.   I have faith in what _ I

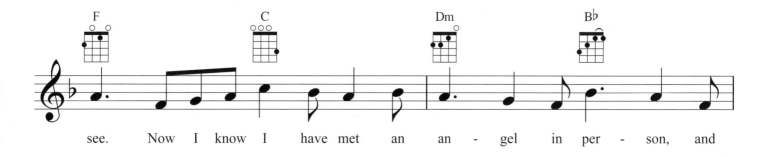

see.   Now I know I   have met   an   an - gel in per - son, and

she   looks per - fect. I don't de - serve this,   you   look   per - fect to-night.

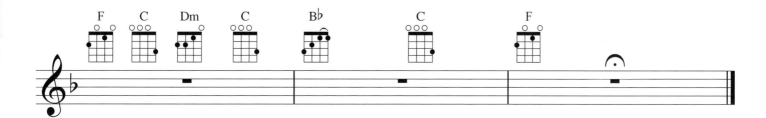

7 Rings

Words and Music by Richard Rodgers, Oscar Hammerstein II, Ariana Grande, Victoria McCants,
Kimberly Krysiuk, Tayla Parx, Tommy Brown, Njomza Vitia, Michael Foster and Charles Anderson

Rath - er be tied up with cuffs and not strings. Write my own checks like I
They say, "Which one?" I say, "Nah, I want all them." Hap - pi - ness is the same

Pre-Chorus

write what I sing. My wrist, stop watch - ing, my neck is floss - ing. Make
price as red bot - toms. My smile is beam - ing, my skin is gleam- ing. The

big de - pos - its, my gloss is pop - ping. You like my hair? Gee,
way it shine, _ I know you've seen it. I bought a crib just

thanks, just bought it. I see it, I like it, I want it, I got it, yeah. I
for the clos - et. Both his _ and hers, _ }

𝄋 Chorus

want it, I got it. I want it, I got it. I want it, I got it. I

117

Shoot, go from the store to the booth, make it all back in one loop. Give me the

loot; nev-er mind, I got the juice. Noth-ing but net when we shoot. Look at my

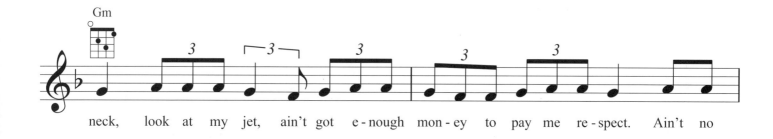

neck, look at my jet, ain't got e-nough mon-ey to pay me re-spect. Ain't no

D.S. al Coda

bud-get when I'm on the set. If I like it, then that's what I get, yeah. I

Outro

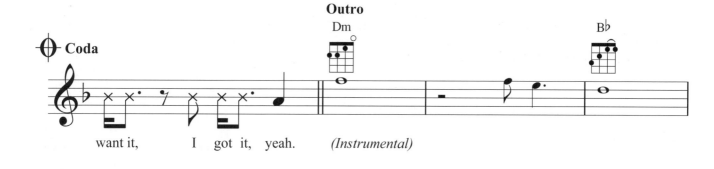

want it, I got it, yeah. *(Instrumental)*

Shallow

from A STAR IS BORN

Words and Music by Stefani Germanotta, Mark Ronson, Andrew Wyatt and Anthony Rossomando

* *Male vocal written at sung pitch.*

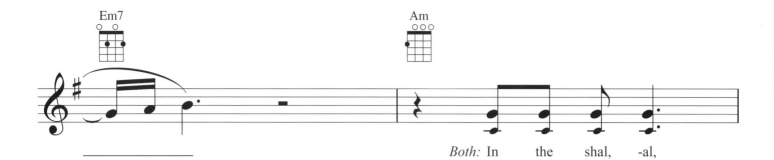

Both: In the shal, -al,

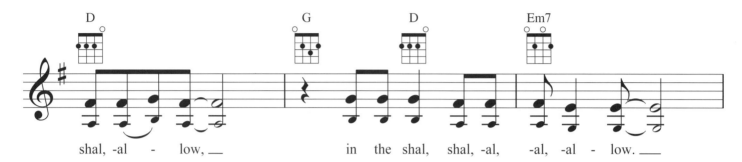

shal, -al - low, ___ in the shal, shal, -al, -al, -al - low. ___

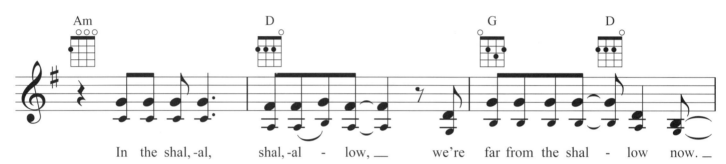

In the shal, -al, shal, -al - low, ___ we're far from the shal - low now. ___

Bridge

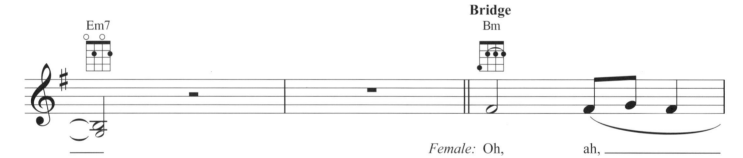

Female: Oh, ah, ___

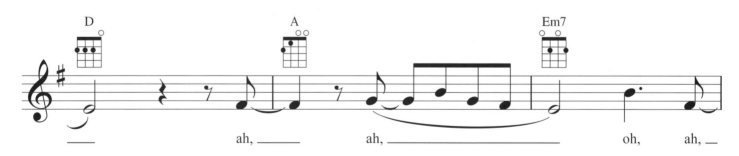

ah, ___ ah, ___ oh, ah, __

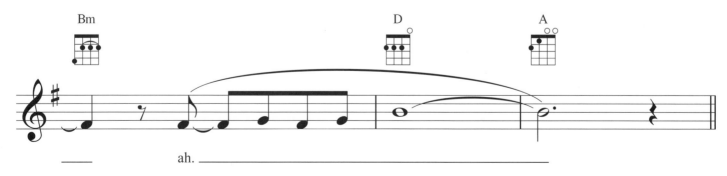

___ ah. ___

Chorus

I'm off the deep ____ end. Watch as I dive ____ in:

I'll nev - er meet ___ the ground. _____ Crash through the sur - face,

where they can't hurt ___ us. We're far from the shal - low now. _____

Both: In the shal, -al, shal - low, __ in the shal, __ shal, -al,

-al, -al - low. __ In the shal, -al, shal - low, __ we're

far from the shal - low now. __

Shape of You

Words and Music by Ed Sheeran, Kevin Briggs, Kandi Burruss,
Tameka Cottle, Steve Mac and Johnny McDaid

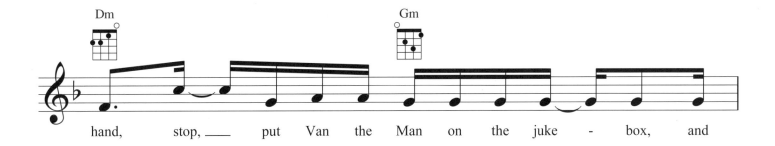

hand, stop, ___ put Van the Man on the juke - box, and

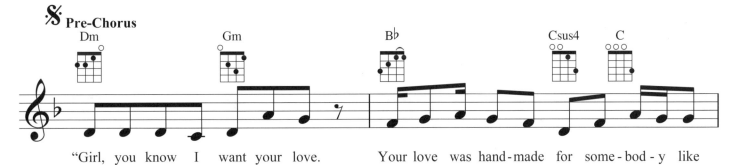

then we start to dance. ___ And now I'm sing - ing like,

𝄋 Pre-Chorus

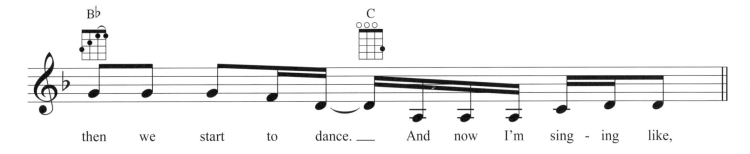

"Girl, you know I want your love. Your love was hand-made for some-bod-y like

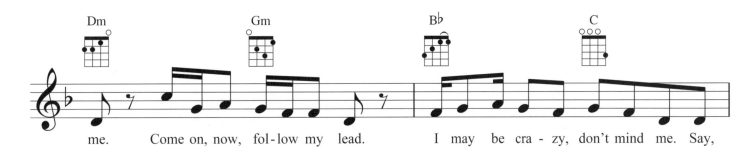

me. Come on, now, fol-low my lead. I may be cra - zy, don't mind me. Say,

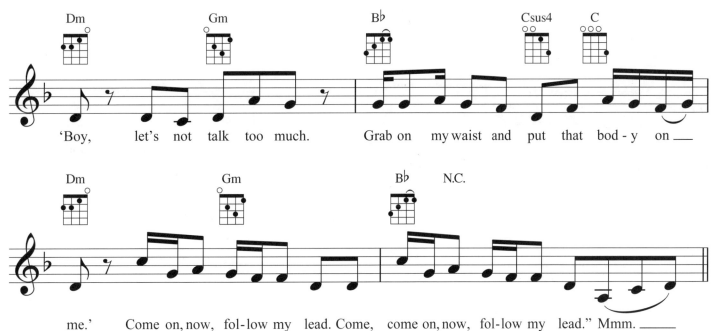

'Boy, let's not talk too much. Grab on my waist and put that bod-y on ___

me.' Come on, now, fol-low my lead. Come, come on, now, fol-low my lead." Mmm. ___

Chorus

(Oh, I, oh, I, oh, I, oh, I.) Well, I'm in love with your bod - y. ___

___ Ev-'ry day dis-cov-er - ing some-thing brand - new. I'm in love with the shape of

Verse

you. 2. One week in, ___ we let the sto - ry be - gin, ___ we're go - ing

out on our first date. ___ You and me are thrift - y, so go "all you can eat," ___ fill up your

bag and I fill up a plate. We talk for hours and hours ___ a - bout sweet and the sour, ___ and how your

fam-i-ly's do-ing o-kay, and leave and get in a tax - i, then kiss in the back ___ seat 'til the

Something Just Like This

Words and Music by Andrew Taggart, Chris Martin, Guy Berryman, Jonny Buckland and Will Champion

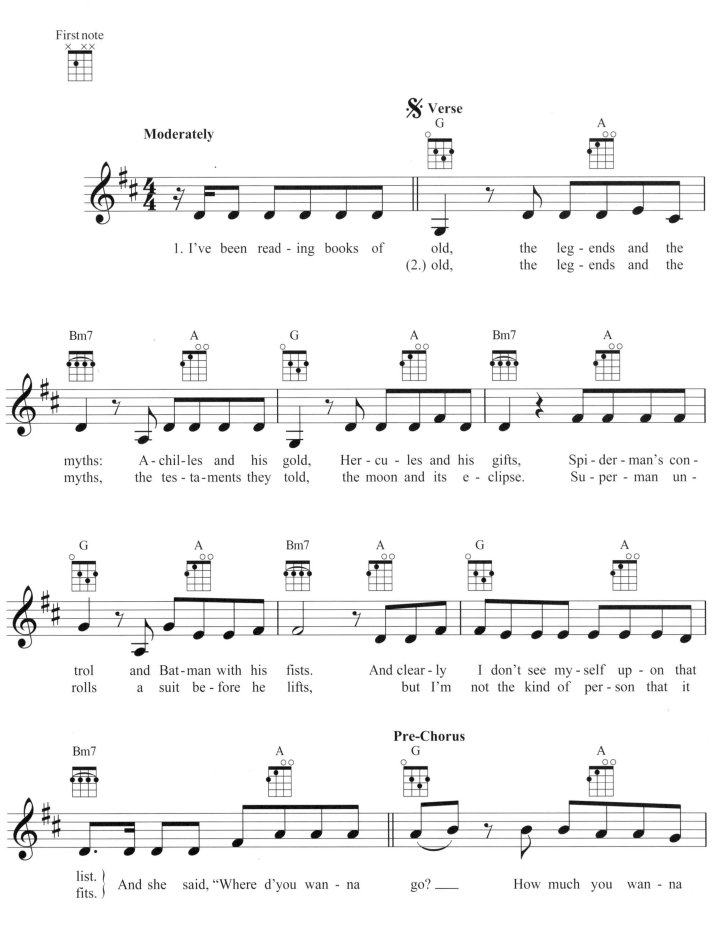

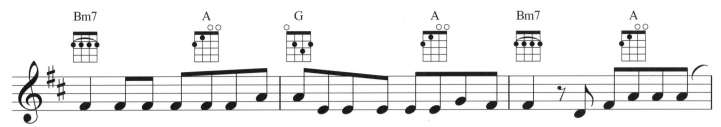

risk? I'm not look-ing for some-bod-y with some su-per-hu-man gifts, some su-per-he-ro, __

To Coda ⊕

__ some fair-y-tale __ bliss. Just some-thing I can turn to, some-bod-y I can

Chorus

kiss. I want some-thing just like ____ this. Do do do do do do, _____ do do do do, _____

____ do do do do do do. Oh, I want some-thing just like __

____ this. Do do do do do do, _____ do do do do, _____ do do do do do do.

Oh, I want some-thing just like _____ this.

Outro

Where d'you wan-na go? How much you wan-na risk? I'm not look-ing for some-

bod-y with some su-per-hu-man gifts, some su-per-he-ro, some fair-y-tale

bliss. Just some-thing I can turn to, some-bod-y I can kiss. I want some-thing just like

this.

Oh, I want some-thing just like this.

Stay

**Words and Music by Alessia Caracciolo, Anders Frøen, Jonnali Parmenius,
Sarah Aarons, Anton Zaslavski and Linus Wiklund**

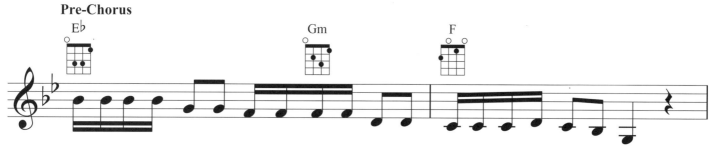

make it on your own, but we don't have to grow up, we can stay for - ev - er young.
make it on my own, but I don't wan - na grow up, we can stay for - ev - er young.

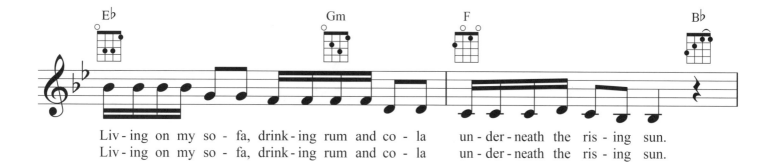

Liv - ing on my so - fa, drink - ing rum and co - la un - der - neath the ris - ing sun.
Liv - ing on my so - fa, drink - ing rum and co - la un - der - neath the ris - ing sun.

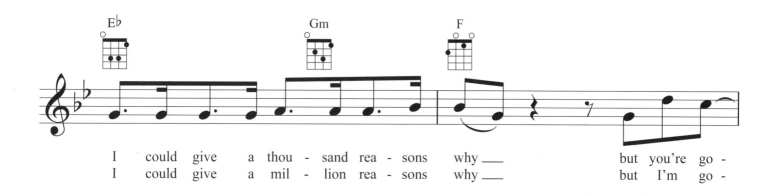

I could give a thou - sand rea - sons why ____ but you're go -
I could give a mil - lion rea - sons why ____ but I'm go -

- ing, and you know ____ that ___ all you have to do is
- ing, and you know ____ that ___

% Chorus

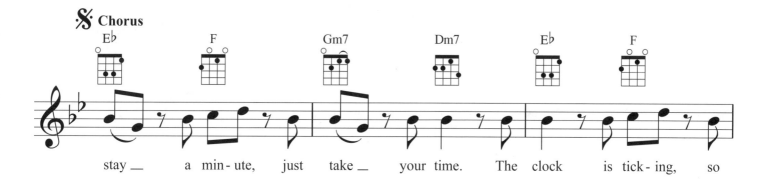

stay __ a min - ute, just take __ your time. The clock is tick - ing, so

135

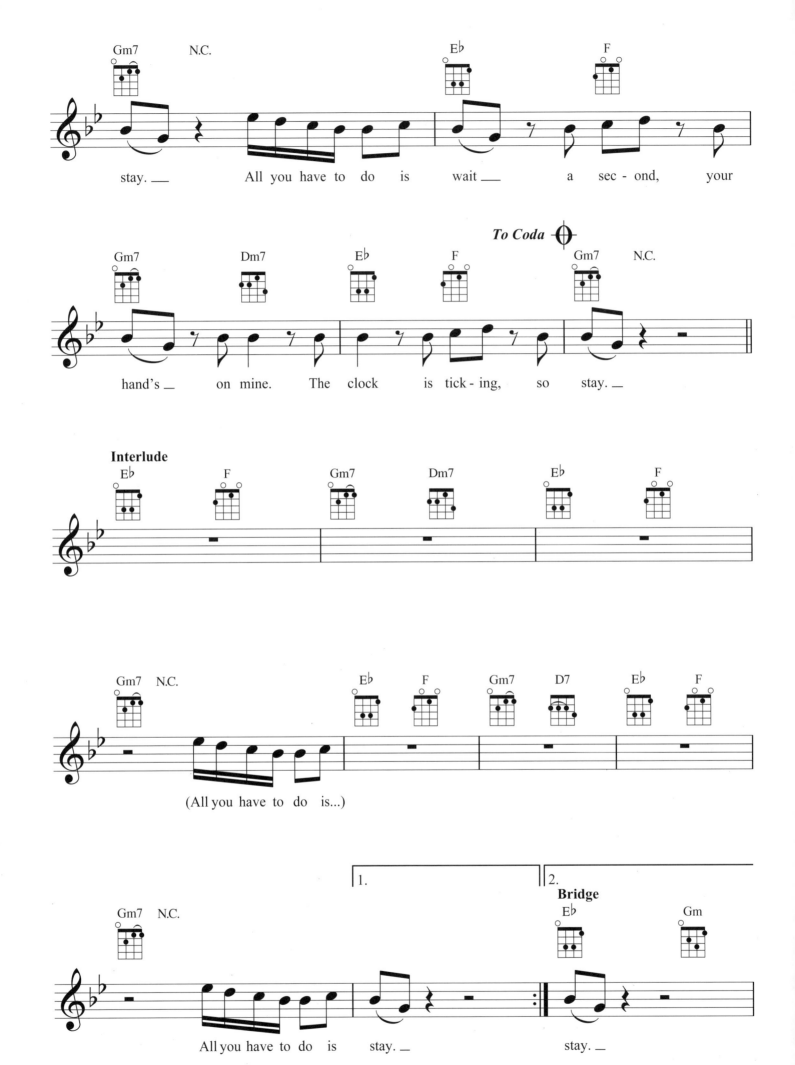

stay. ___   All you have to do is wait ___ a sec - ond, your

To Coda

hand's ___ on mine. The clock is tick - ing, so stay. ___

Interlude

(All you have to do is...)

1.

2.   **Bridge**

All you have to do is stay. ___   stay. ___

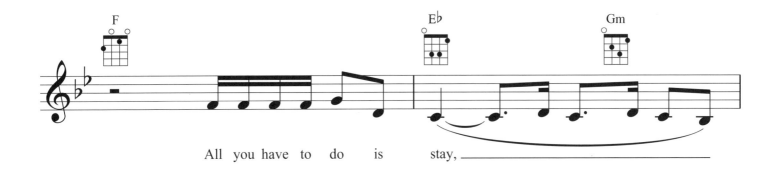

All you have to do is stay, _____

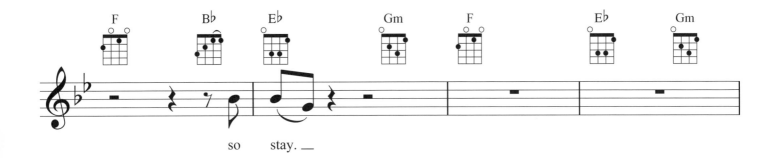

so stay. _

D.S. al Coda

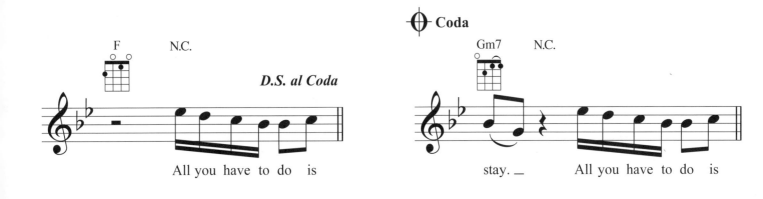

All you have to do is

⊕ **Coda**

stay. _ All you have to do is

Outro

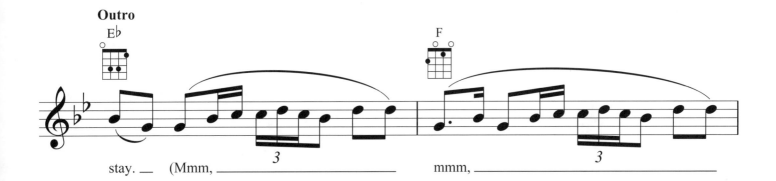

stay. _ (Mmm, _____ mmm, _____

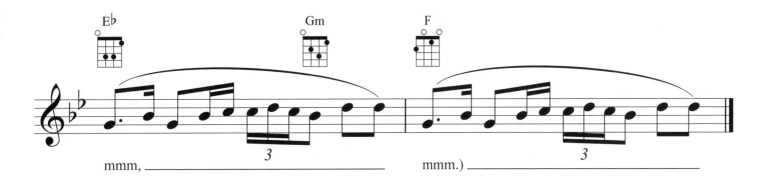

mmm, _____ mmm.) _____

137

Sucker

Words and Music by Nick Jonas, Joseph Jonas, Carl Rosen,
Ryan Tedder, Louis Bell, Adam Feeney and Kevin Jonas

Without Me

Words and Music by Ashley Frangipane, Brittany Amaradio, Carl Rosen, Justin Timberlake, Scott Storch, Louis Bell, Amy Allen and Timothy Mosley

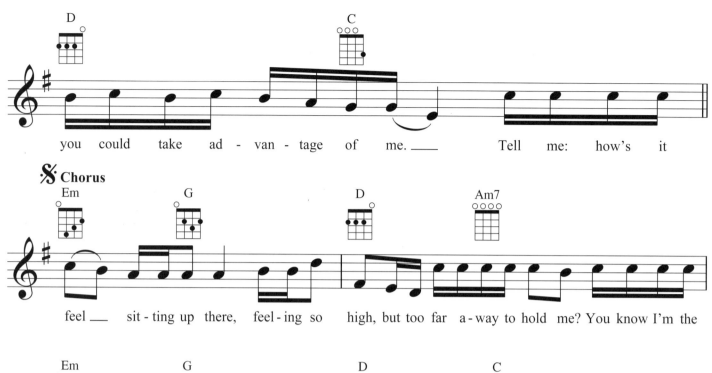

you could take ad - van - tage of me. ___ Tell me: how's it

%Chorus

feel ___ sit - ting up there, feel - ing so high, but too far a - way to hold me? You know I'm the

one who put you up there, name in the sky; does it ev - er get lone - ly think - ing you could

live _____ with - out ___ me, ___ think - ing you could

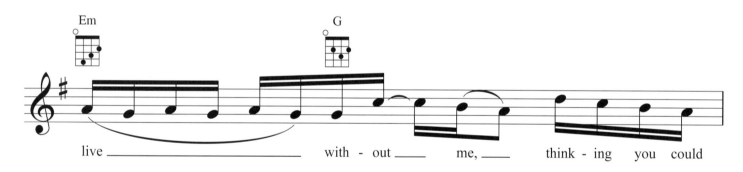

live _____ with - out ___ me? Ba - by, I'm the

To Coda ✛

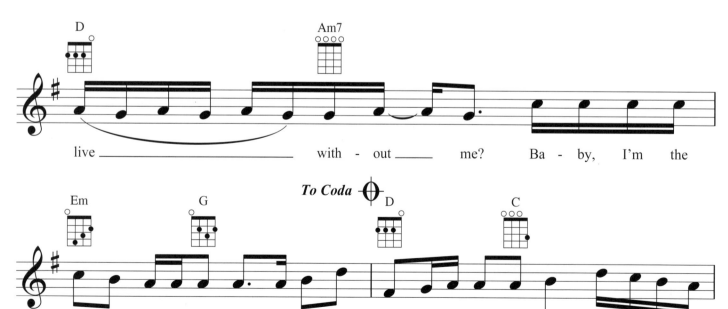

one who put you up there. I don't know why.(Yeah, I don't know why.) Think - ing you could

live _____ with - out _____ me, _____

live _____ with - out _____ me. Ba - by, I'm the

one who put you up there. I don't know why. _

why, _ yeah. _

Bridge

You don't have to say just what you did; I

al - read - y know. I had to go and find out from them. _ So tell me: how's it

N.C.

D.S. al Coda

feel? _ Tell me: how's it

Coda

why. (Yeah, I don't know why.)

Sunflower

from SPIDER-MAN: INTO THE SPIDER-VERSE

**Words and Music by Austin Richard Post, Carl Austin Rosen,
Khalif Brown, Carter Lang, Louis Bell and Billy Walsh**

Some-one took a big L, don't know how that felt. _ Look-ing at you side-ways, par-ty on tilt.

Pre-Chorus

Ooh, _____ some things you just can't re - fuse. _____ She wan-na

ride like a cruise, _____ and I'm not tryin' to lose. _____

Chorus

Then you're left in the dust un - less I stuck by ya.

You're the sun - flow - er. I think your love would be too much,

or you'll be left in the dust un - less I stuck by ya. You're the sun - flow - er,

Outro-Chorus

but it's out of my con-trol. _____ Then you'll be left in the dust

un-less I stuck by ya. You're the sun-flow - er.

I think your love would be too much, or you'll be left in the dust

un-less I stuck by ya. You're the sun-flow - er,

you're the sun-flow - er.

Sweet but Psycho

Words and Music by Amanda Koci, Andreas Haukeland,
William Lobban Bean, Henry Walter and Madison Love

151

Thank U, Next

Words and Music by Ariana Grande, Victoria McCants, Kimberly Krysiuk,
Tayla Parx, Tommy Brown, Charles Anderson and Michael Foster

thank - ful. Wish I could say "thank you" to Mal - colm, _ 'cause he was an
last, ____ 'cause her name is Ar - i, ____ and I'm so good with
last. ____ God for - bid some-thing hap - pens. _ 'Least this song is a

Pre-Chorus

an - gel. __ One taught _ me love, one taught _ me
that. _____ She taught _ me love, she taught _ me
smash. _____ I've got so ___ much love, got so ___ much

pa - tience, _ and one taught _ me pain. Now I'm so ___ a -
pa - tience. _ How she han - dles pain, that shit's _ a -
pa - tience. _ I've learned from ___ the pain. It turned out ___ a -

mazed as ___ I've loved and ___ I've lost. But that's not ___ what
maz - ing. ___ I've loved and ___ I've lost, but that's not ___ what
maz - ing. ___ I've loved and ___ I've lost, but that's not ___ what

I see, ___ so look what ___ I got. Look what ___ you
I see, ___ 'cause look what ___ I found. No need ___ for
I see, ___ 'cause look what ___ I found. No need ___ for

Chorus

taught me. ___
search - ing. ___
search - ing. ___

And ___ for ___ that ___ I ___ say: Thank u, ___ next,

next. Thank u, ___ next, next. Thank u, ___ next. I'm so fuck-ing grate-ful for my

To Coda

ex. Thank u, ___ next, next. Thank u, ___ next, next. Thank u, ___ next.

1.

I'm so fuck - ing... 2. Spend more time with my

2.

I'm so fuck-ing grate-ful for my

Bridge

ex. Thank u, next. ___

Thank u, next. ___

Bm7   D7   *D.S. al Coda*

Thank u, next. _____ I'm so fuck - ing... 3. One day I'll walk down that

D7   **Bridge**
          Gmaj7

Coda

I'm so fuck-ing grate-ful for my ex. Thank u, next. _____

A#°7   Bm7   D7

Thank u, next. ___ Thank u, next. _____ Yeah, ee.

Gmaj7   A#°7   Bm7

Thank u, next. ___ Thank u, next. ___ Thank u, next. _____

Outro   *Repeat and fade*
D7   Gmaj7   A#°7   Bm7   D7

Yeah, ee. *(Instrumental)*

That's What I Like

Words and Music by Bruno Mars, Philip Lawrence, James Fauntleroy, Ray Charles McCullough II, Christopher Brody Brown, Jeremy Reeves, Jonathan Yip and Ray Romulus

(just to put a smile on it.) You de-serve it, ba-by, you de - serve it all; _____ and

Chorus

I'm gon-na give it to you. Gold jew'l-ry shin-ing so bright; straw - ber - ry

cham - pagne on ice. Luck-y for you, that's what I like, that's what I like.

Luck-y for you, that's what I like, that's what I like. Sex by the

fi - re at night; silk sheets and dia-monds, all white. Luck-y for you, that's what I

like, that's what I like. Luck-y for you, that's what I like, that's what I like.

158

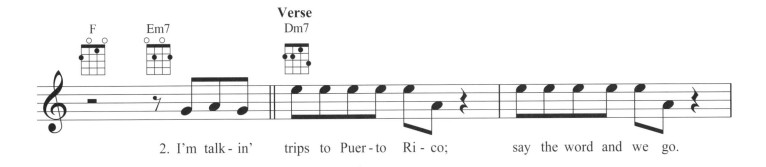

Verse

2. I'm talk-in' trips to Puer-to Ri-co; say the word and we go.

You can be my freek-a; girl, I'll be a flee-ko, *ma - ma -*

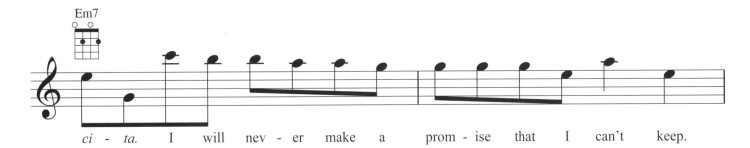

ci - ta. I will nev - er make a prom - ise that I can't keep.

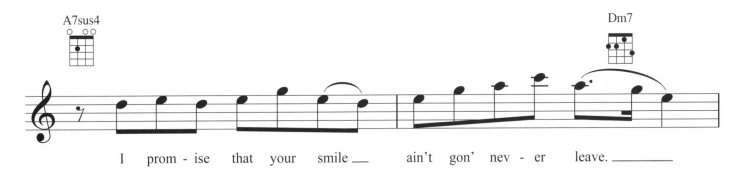

I prom - ise that your smile ___ ain't gon' nev - er leave. ___

Shop - ping sprees in Par - is; ev - 'ry - thing twen - ty - four kar - ats.

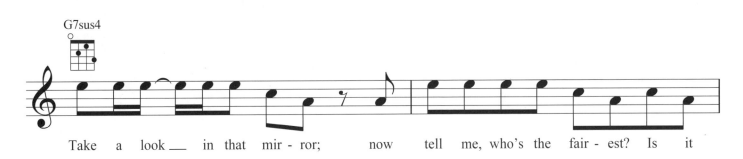

Take a look ___ in that mir - ror; now tell me, who's the fair - est? Is it

There's Nothing Holdin' Me Back

Words and Music by Shawn Mendes, Geoffrey Warburton, Teddy Geiger and Scott Harris

1. I want to fol-low where she goes,
2. She says that she's nev-er a-fraid;

I think a-bout her and she knows it. _____
just pic-ture ev-'ry-bod-y na-ked. _____

I want to let her take con-
She real-ly does-n't like to

trol,
wait,

'cause ev-'ry time that she gets clos-er, she
not real-ly in-to hes-i-ta-tion.

pulls }
Pulls } me in e-nough to keep __ me guess - ing. Mm. __

_____ May-be I should stop and start con-fess-

-ing, con-fess - ing, yeah. _____ Oh, I've been shak-ing, I love

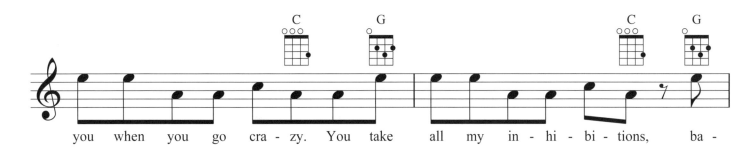

you when you go cra-zy. You take all my in - hi - bi - tions, ba -

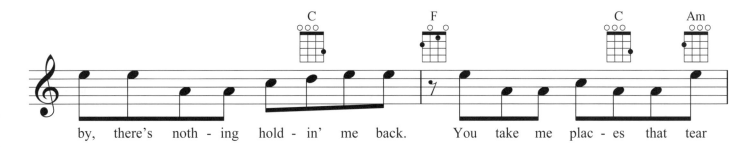

by, there's noth-ing hold-in' me back. You take me plac-es that tear

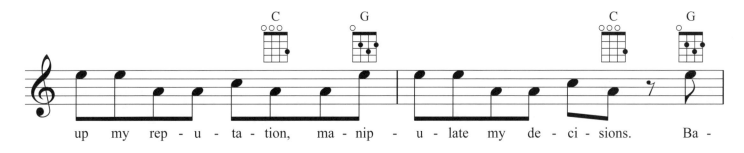

up my rep - u - ta - tion, ma - nip - u - late my de - ci - sions. Ba -

Interlude

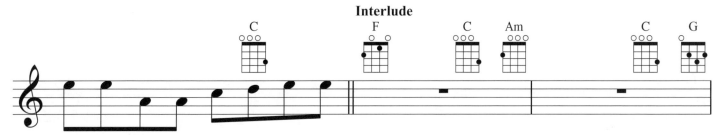

by, there's noth - ing hold - in' me back.

To Coda

There's noth - ing hold - in' me back.

1.

There's noth-ing hold-in' me back.

2.   **Bridge**

'Cause if we lost our minds and we took __

__ it way too far, I know we'd be al - right, I know we __

__ would be al - right. If you were by my side and we stum-

- bled in the dark, I know we'd be al - right, I know we __

__ would be al - right. 'Cause if we lost our minds and we took __

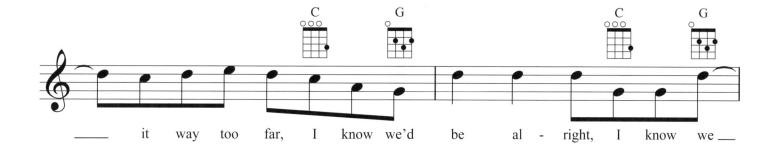

_____ it way too far, I know we'd be al - right, I know we _____

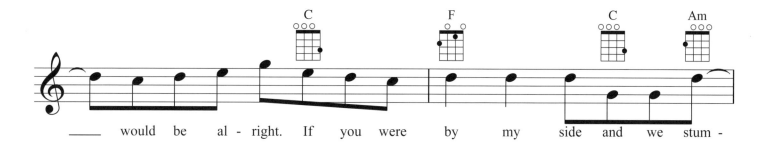

_____ would be al - right. If you were by my side and we stum -

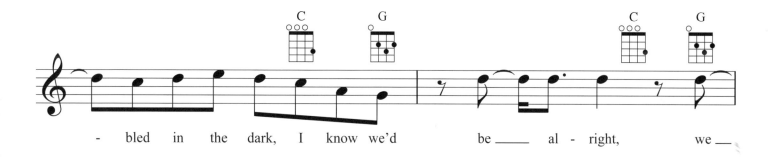

- bled in the dark, I know we'd be _____ al - right, we _____

D.S. al Coda

_____ would be al - right. _____

✛ **Coda**

There's noth - ing hold - in' me back.

Outro

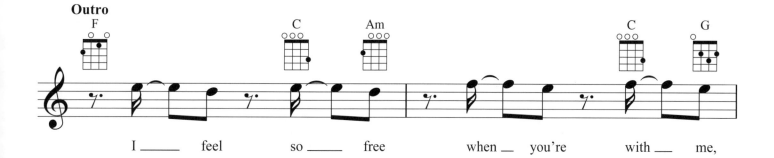

I _____ feel so _____ free when _____ you're with _____ me,

ba - by. Ba - by, there's noth - ing hold - in' me back. _____

Thunder

Words and Music by Dan Reynolds, Wayne Sermon, Ben McKee,
Daniel Platzman, Alexander Grant and Jayson DeZuzio

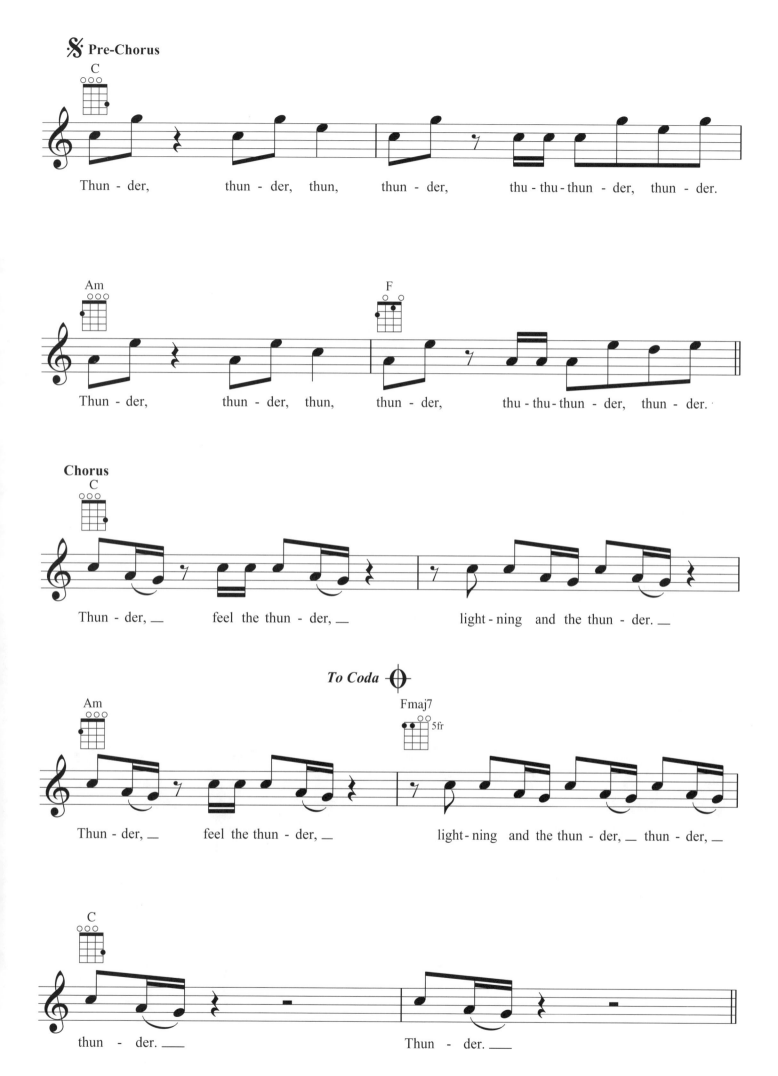

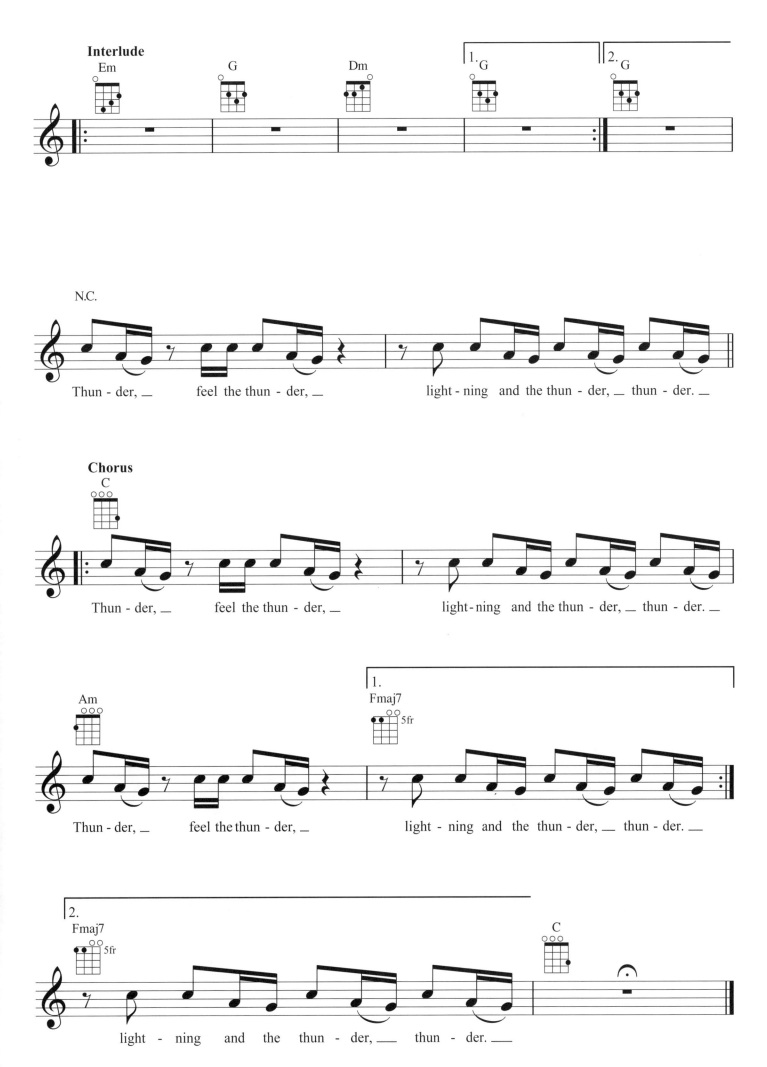

Too Good at Goodbyes

Words and Music by Sam Smith, Tor Hermansen,
Mikkel Eriksen and James Napier

ev - 'ry time I o - pen up, it hurts. _____ So I'm

nev - er gon - na get too close to you, e - ven when I mean the most to you, in

case you go and leave me in the dirt. But ev - 'ry time you

Chorus

hurt me, the less that I cry. ____ And ev - 'ry time you leave me, the quick - er these tears _

____ dry. And ev - 'ry time you walk out, the less I love you. ____ Ba - by, we don't stand a

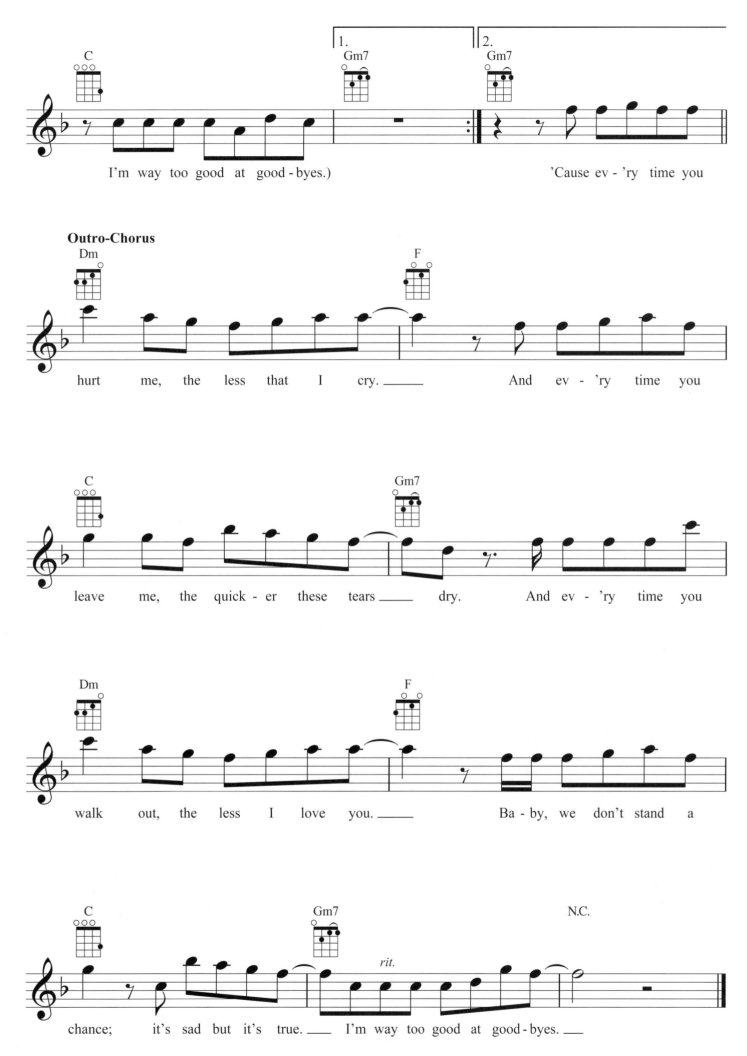

Outro-Chorus

What Lovers Do

**Words and Music by Adam Levine, Solána Rowe, Jason Evigan,
Oladayo Olatunji, Brittany Hazzard, Victor Raadstrom and Ben Diehl**

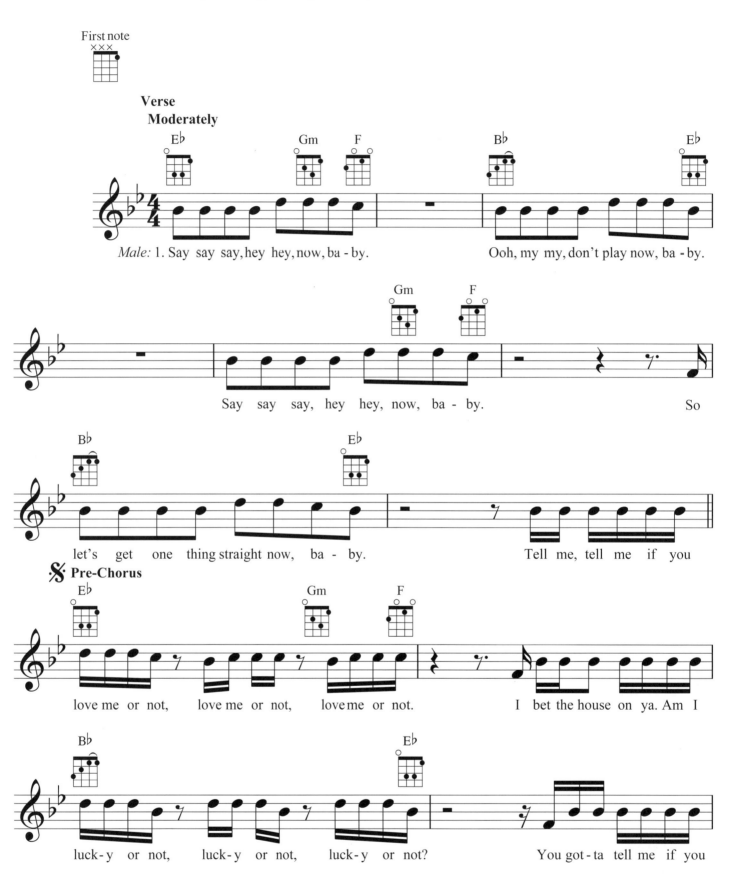

love me or not,   love me or not,   love me or not.   Been wish-ing for ya. Am I

luck - y   or not,   luck - y   or not,   luck - y   or not?

Chorus

Ooh ooh ooh ooh ooh, __ been wish - ing for you, __   ooh, __ ooh, __ try - na do what

lov - ers do, __   ooh. __   Ooh ooh ooh ooh ooh, __ been wish - ing for you, __   ooh, __

To Coda

ooh, __   try - na do what lov - ers do, __   ooh. __ 2. Say say say, hey hey, now, ba - by.

Female:

Verse

You gon' make me hit you with that lay down, ba - by.

175

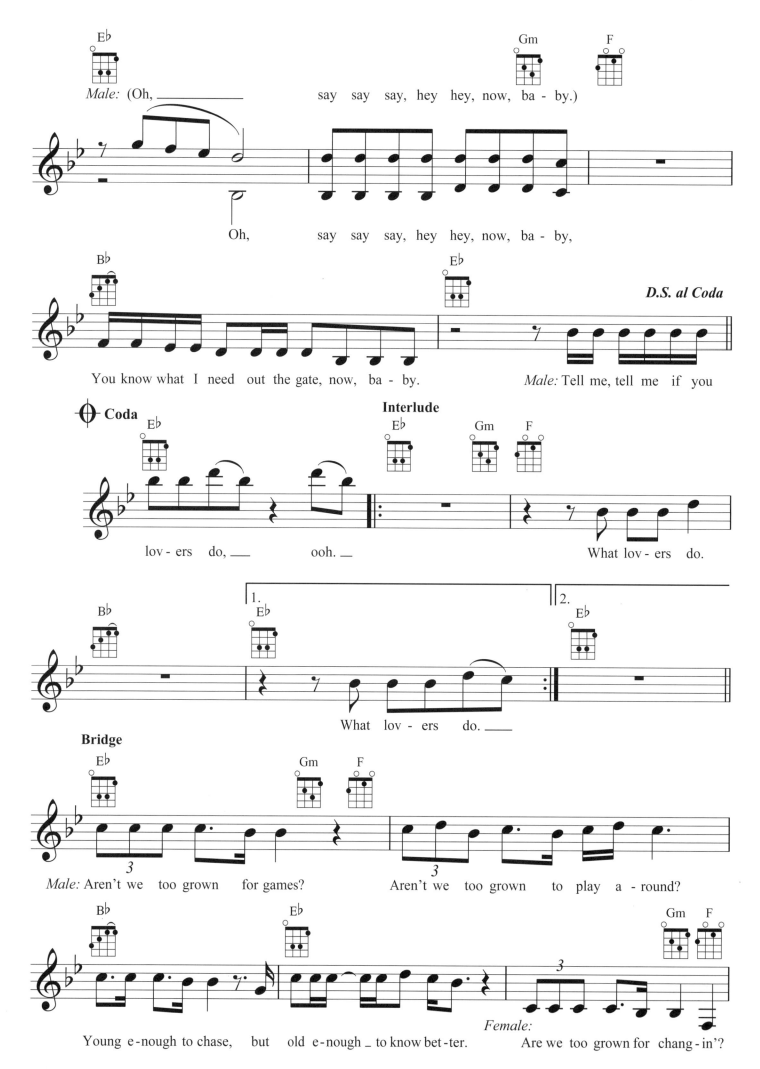

Male: (Oh, _____ say say say, hey hey, now, ba - by.)

Oh, _____ say say say, hey hey, now, ba - by,

You know what I need out the gate, now, ba - by.

D.S. al Coda

Male: Tell me, tell me if you

Coda

Interlude

lov - ers do, ____ ooh. ___

What lov - ers do.

1.

What lov - ers do. ___

2.

Bridge

Male: Aren't we too grown for games?

Aren't we too grown to play a - round?

Young e - nough to chase, but old e - nough _ to know bet - ter.

Female:

Are we too grown for chang - in'?

Are we too grown to mess a-round? _ And, ooh, and now can't wait for-ev-er, ba - by.

Chorus

Both of us ____ should know bet - ter.

Male:

Ooh ooh ooh ooh ooh, _ been wish - ing for you, _ ooh, _

ooh, _ try - na do what lov-ers do, _ ooh. _

Outro-Chorus

Ooh ooh ooh ooh ooh, _ been wish - ing for you, _ ooh, _ ooh, _ try - na do what

lov-ers do, ___ ooh. _ Ooh ooh ooh ooh ooh, _ been wish - ing for you, _ ooh, _

1.

ooh, _ try - na do what lov-ers do, _ ooh. _

2.

lov-ers do, _ ooh. _

Wolves

Words and Music by Selena Gomez, Carl Rosen,
Andrew Wotman, Ali Tamposi, Louis Bell and Marshmello

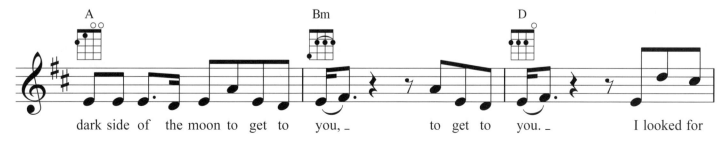

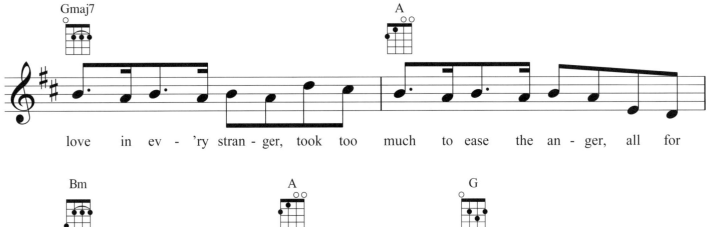

love in ev - 'ry stran - ger, took too much to ease the an - ger, all for

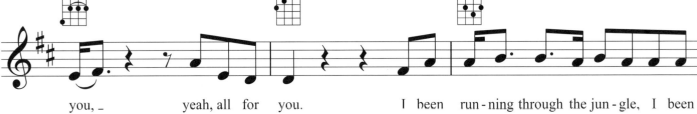

you, ___ yeah, all for you. I been run - ning through the jun - gle, I been

cry - ing with the wolves to get to you, ___ to get to you, _____ to get to

Interlude

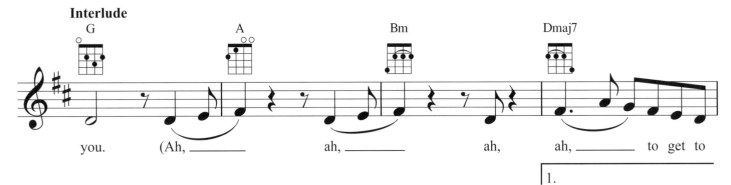

you. (Ah, _____ ah, _____ ah, ah, _____ to get to

you. Ah, _____ ah, _____ ah, ah, _____ to get to

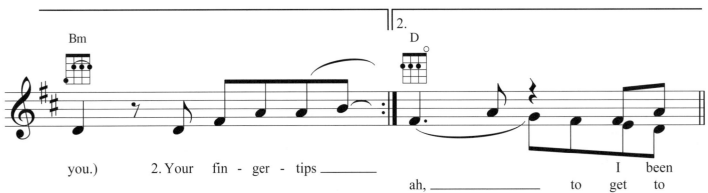

you.) 2. Your fin - ger - tips _____

I been

ah, _____ to get to

Outro-Chorus

run - ning through the jun - gle, I been run - ning with the wolves to get to you.)

you, __ to get to you. __ I been down the dark - est al - leys, saw the

dark side of the moon to get to you, __ to get to you. I looked for

love in ev - 'ry stran - ger, took too much to ease the an - ger, all for you, __ yeah, all for

you. I been run - ning through the jun - gle, I been cry - ing with the wolves to get to

you, __ to get to you, _____ to get to you.

Young, Dumb and Broke

Words and Music by Khalid Robinson, Joel Little and Talay Riley

First note

Verse
Moderately slow

G

1. So, you're still think-ing of me, just like I know you should.
2. We have so much in com-mon, we ar-gue all the time.

Em   **D**

I can-not give you ev-'ry-thing; you know I wish I could.
You al-ways say I'm wrong; _____ I'm pret-ty sure I'm right.

G

(1., 3.) I'm so high at the mo-ment, I'm so caught up in this.
(2.) What's fun a-bout com-mit-ment when we have our life to live?

Em   **D**

Yeah, we're just young, dumb and broke, but we still got love to give while we're

Chorus

young, dumb, young, young, _ dumb and broke. ___ Young, dumb, young, young, _ dumb and broke.

Young, dumb, young, young, _ dumb and broke. ___ Young, dumb, broke high school kids.

Ya - da - da - da - da - da - da - da. ___ Ya - da - da - da - da - da - da.

Ya - da - da - da - da - da - da - da. Young, dumb, broke high school kids.

Bridge

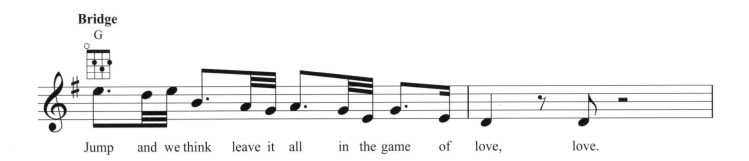

Jump and we think leave it all in the game of love, love.

D.S. al Coda
(no repeat)

Run in-to sin, do it all in the name of fun, fun. Whoa - oa - oa.

Outro

Coda

Ya - da - da - da - da - da - da - da. __ Ya - da - da - da - da - da - da.

Ya - da - da - da da - da - da - da. Young, dumb, broke high school kids.